The Millenium Church

A Now Prophetic Word To The Body Of Christ

REV. MRS. KATHY SANDLIN

WESTBOW®
PRESS
A DIVISION OF THOMAS NELSON
& ZONDERVAN

WestBow Press books may be ordered through booksellers or by contacting:

WestBow Press
A Division of Thomas Nelson & Zondervan
1663 Liberty Drive
Bloomington, IN 47403
www.westbowpress.com
1 (866) 928-1240

ISBN: 978-1-4908-5167-9 (sc)
ISBN: 978-1-4908-5168-6 (e)

Library of Congress Control Number: 2014916324

Printed in the United States of America.

WestBow Press rev. date: 9/18/2014

CONTENTS

DEDICATION

This book is dedicated to all the pastors and leaders of America and around the World operating in five-fold ministry who are raising up Millennium Churches in this hour.

ACKNOWLEDGEMENTS

I would like to thank my staff and ministry team
The International Cathedral of Prayer for their loving
support, encouragement and much more valued
intercession over the writing of this work.

I would like to thank both Melanie Riddle for her
editing skills and Elisha Oles for her typesetting
skills and techniques on this project.

STATEMENTS OF ENDORSEMENT

As each of us had come to learn in life, there comes a time when the spiritual and practical will work hand in hand. You, like me, have probably read a lot of great church growth material which focuses greatly on the practical without much spiritual insight. In this book I feel that Kathy has given us a deep spiritual look into the future church, along with tools of practical implication. We must always believe God is birthing something new in us.

Rev. Derrick G. Gardner, Sr. Pastor
Life Springs Worship Center, Lexington, SC

As Apostolic Pastors planting church in Europe, we are confident that you will not want to miss the prophetic insights that God has given to Prophetess Kathy Sandlin for The Millennium Church described within this book. As these paradigm shifts are implemented and take place, God will break through mightily! Then the church will affect our world and bring in the last day harvest!

Pastors Bert & Melodee Phagan
Praise Center, Brussels, Belgium

It is an honor to place my endorsement upon this book, *"The Millennium Church."* This special Lady of Grace has been called forth by God as a Prophetess to the Nations. The book is filled with *Prophetic Instruction* that will catapult the church into a brand new dimension of a mighty move of the Holy Spirit! As I read this book, I found myself with desire to do more than pastor an *organization* that the Father breathes upon, but to passionately pastor an *organism* that the Father breathes through.

David Oxley, Sr.
Calvary Christian Fellowship, Oklahoma City, OK

The Millennium Church is an excellent text, which provides significant insight into the purpose and pattern of the much-needed 21st Century Church. Prophetess Kathy Sandlin brings important revelation of prophetic insight to the Body of Christ which alerts us to our divine call and duty. This book will equip the Church to achieve its maximum impact.

Garry Bryant, Superintendent
Redemption Ministries, International Pentecostal Holiness Church, Eastern Virginia

The Millennium Church is a book for the church of today and tomorrow. An invaluable tool to help leadership and laity understand how God is suitably adapting His Church for unity in history's greatest hour of Harvest. It echo's Revelation 3:22, "He that hath an ear, let him hear what the Spirit saith unto the churches."

Dr. David E. Hayes, Pastor
Family Worship & Praise Center, Hopewell, Virginia

INTRODUCTION

Psalm 45: 1&2 says, "My heart is stirred by a noble theme as I recite my verses for the King; my tongue is a pen of a skilled writer. You are the most excellent of people and your lips have been anointed with grace, since God has blessed you forever." (The Leadership Bible, NIV)

These two verses express the criteria of my heart as I have written for you this book entitled "The Millennium Church." That which began as a four-point sermon outline, has turned into twelve chapters of a revelatory, *Prophetic* word for the body of Christ both now and in the days to come. In this writing I have made every possible effort to captivate, embrace, and express that which I see with a Prophetic eye for the last day move of God in and through our churches. All around the world there is a move of the Holy Spirit that is revolutionizing the Body of Christ and comparable to none which we have experienced in the past.

Yet the coming move of God that is on the horizon will far supersede the Azusa Street Revival, along with all of the present day outpourings that are taking place. This synopsis of the third day church, The Millennium Church, is exciting and exhilarating to the spirit of man, and I believe will help to raise up a new breed of people who will be drawn together by the Holy Spirit, to welcome and embrace this powerfully unique New Testament Church! Jesus said, "If I be lifted up from the earth, I will draw all men unto me." If we are going to reach the population of the world for Christ, we must prepare to make Jesus the center of attention and the main attraction in our fellowships.

We must be willing to change our mindsets and continue to do things differently than ever before. We must also pray for the grace that we will need to set the flesh aside and be led by the Holy Spirit as we lead these Millennium Churches to victory!

Spiritual Maturity is not an option. It is a necessity! God is looking for an army, not a nursery! Lambs do not feed lambs. Sheep feed lambs. We must grow up and mature. The church must arise in this hour. We are definitely living in the Holy Spirit dispensation and this is His day!

We must be: Millennial; conducive to the will of God for this day and for this hour.

Model; setting an example so that others will want to pattern their ministries and churches after ours. Maternal; being willing to give birth to daughter churches on a continual basis. Mobile; purpose to be movable – when the cloud moves we must move and when the cloud stops, we must stop! Mighty; a spiritual warfare mentality will be that which will pull this last day church to the forefront. Militant; clothed with the whole armor of God and ready for battle!

Musical; people of praise and worship that will know how to usher in the presence of the Lord and honor Him once He gets there! Multiethnic; understanding that we are all created in the image of God and if we turn ethnic groups away from our doors, it will be as though we are turning God away from our church doors as well. Meticulous; extremely careful to attend to details in caring about the most important things and making sure that they have priority. Miraculous; filled with those who will be shadow casters and impart healing as we walk the streets of our cities. Multiple; all areas should and will experience increase. And finally, The Maiden Church; a Church Bride that will adorn herself, and passionately long for intimate spiritual relationship with her Bridegroom!

As you read this book my prayer is that God will enhance your vision, sharpen your skills, impart greater wisdom, equip you for the work of the ministry, put new fire in your spirit, and release the five-fold ministry gift or gifts within you that we may all work together as one to build The New Millennium Church for the glory of the Lord! You may not agree with all of it. Parts of it may rub against our religious grain. However, we may all receive parts of it for the building of the Body of Christ!

We must never be afraid to implement new things for the Kingdom of God. The Red Sea might not have parted if Moses had not raised his hand. Peter would have never recognized his dependency upon Jesus if he had not gotten out of the boat. Esther would have never known her level of favor with the King if she had not taken a chance! Hannah might never have prayed a desperate prayer had she allowed herself to be intimidated by Eli. Millennium Churches will be made up of kingdom people. Millennium Church pastors and leaders will be composed of kingdom personnel. We must be willing to take a chance. We must never be afraid to step out! *What God employs us to do, He will empower us for!*

When I was a little girl, I lived with my grandparents. My granddaddy worked in a cotton mill and my grandmother was an industrious housewife. She always cooked two times a day. Breakfast was imperative for my granddaddy and she prepared supper for us around four o'clock every afternoon. She was a tremendous cook and liked to try new recipes. It would make me very nervous because she expected everyone to eat what she prepared! Whenever I would appear not to have a desire to eat her new recipes, she would say to me, "Kathy, just try it. If you don't like it then leave it on your plate." So I say to you, "Just try it. And if you do not like it, just leave it on your plate!"

Come on Church! Arise, shine, for your light has come and the glory of the Lord has risen upon you. May this book lay a foundation for you and I to build together powerful, effective Millennium Churches!

With great expectations,

Prophetess Kathy Sandlin

CHAPTER 1

The Millennium Church

M uch of today's society entertains a kaleidoscope of concepts regarding what the "Church," or the "Body of Christ", should appear to be, and how she should function. Some people consider the church to be nothing more than a structural, architectural frame, simply a place to house a weekly ritual of worship. They hold on to a material structure because of ancestral heritage. This thing or its people have become sacred cows that have yet to be sacrificed upon the altar before the Lord. Someone in their family may have previously attended, or even started the church. It could be a friend or the Pastor at some point in time. Whatever the case, there is always room for adjustment regarding our concepts of the Church as Christ's Church!

Some of them may appear to be grandiose cathedrals in their outward appearance, and yet the beauty of the outward camouflages a house of dead men's bones. Hidden within the walls of these types of structures are spiritual diseases, that if allowed to remain in us, can restrain us and stagnate our progression in the things of God. These diseases are such things as sectarianism, manipulation, control, pride, politics, greed, and power struggles just to name a few. These are all works of the flesh that will hinder the mighty flow of the Holy Spirit that the Father desires to have operative within His Church, especially in The New Millennium. Over the years, the church has been plagued with many mental, emotional, financial and spiritual beliefs and concepts that have been, and still are, devastating to the Body of Christ.

Unfortunately, these concepts have brought on a spiritual paralysis to the Body of Christ, producing some weak and feeble churches. The diagnosis of some of these churches may read "Terminal". However, I believe that the prognosis is "Recovery". I know without a doubt that there is a desire within the heart of our Heavenly Father to help us understand who we are in and through Him. I believe that He longs to bring clarity and definition to everything that He has designed His Body to be. The Millennium Church will be a people that will cause the world to look and wonder who we are, as well as produce a desire within their very being to become a part of this last day church!

We must keep in mind, that the Church is not a building, but a Body – a Body in which Jesus Christ must be allowed to be the Head. Ephesians 1:22 & 23 says, "And God placed all things under His feet, and appointed Him to be 'HEAD' over everything for the church, which is 'HIS BODY', the fullness of Him, who fills everything in every way."(Leadership Bible, NIV).

I believe in this day more than ever, that Christ has the desire for His church to 'Resemble' Him. To the natural person, nothing makes a Father any more proud than to hear someone say, "Your child looks just like you." It gives that Father such a sense of honor to know by the resemblance and features, that his offspring is both noticeable and recognizable by the beholder as belonging to him. That is the way the church ought to be. We should so resemble the Father that there would be no question as to whom we belong. The head on our body does the thinking, turning, seeing, hearing, planning, and setting in order. He implements movement and is responsible for the healthy functioning of the rest of the body. It is a simple truth, yet so profound, that Christ is the Head and we, the people, make up His body!

The church mentioned in this scripture has reference to being His Body! Ephesians declares to us that His body is the "FULLNESS OF HIM!" That tells me that we must be filled up with 'Him' and not ourselves. Scripture reveals to us that "Blessed are they who hunger and thirst after righteousness, for they shall be filled." The Apostle Paul declares that His Body being the church is the fullness of Him. Whenever we make the statement that we are the Body of Christ, we are declaring that we are willing to fill all of the voids and become all things to all men, that we may by some means gain some, just like the Apostle Paul. The Millennium Church will be willing to bring about change in order to reach as many as possible for the Kingdom of God. Change to The Millennium Church will not become a task; it will be a part of its everyday function.

We desperately need our church programs, but are they bringing forth progress? Praise God for another meeting, but what about ministry? Praise God for bringing the hurting, but did they leave with their healing? Do we make room for the poor, and then give them the opportunity and training to become prosperous? Are the demon- possessed that walk in to our fellowships, leaving delivered by the blood of Jesus? When the sinner walks through the door, do they leave with a Savior, having instantaneously become a new creature? The real Body of Christ fills everything in every way. The Millennium Church will have no problem taking care of these issues, because of the mentality of "filling everything in every way."

Men and women in ministry, and especially pastoral positions, must be ever mindful of allowing Him to be the Head of everything that we are doing in our Churches. We must be very careful not to become performance oriented in our worship and service to the Lord. God is tired of Planned Pentecostal Performance; He is looking for His Holy Spirit to generate within us a Dynamic Power that will carry out His divine mandate! Not only does God expect it, but people in general are looking for it also. With a strong core of church members operating in the power of the Holy Spirit, His Body being in the proper order will began to manifest the fullness of His power and will fill all of the places in our churches where we are lacking as a people of God. There is going to be a transformation in the spirit realm that will enable us to become the true New Millennium Church!

Secondly, we are more than an Organization. We are a living breathing organism. I believe as an organization we should exhibit excellence in all that we do for God's Kingdom. I believe in order, rules and a system. When God created the world, He laid His Hand upon 'Chaos' and brought it to divine order. Everything that God created thereafter He gave specific rules by which to operate. The sun shines by day. The moon and stars glow in the night. There are times that God may interrupt that process and allow the *clouds* to take over. Nevertheless, because man does not control the atmosphere, God orchestrates a divine interruption and still operates within His own system, so that even the clouds will bring Him glory! The clouds are *different* from the sun, moon and stars, but they are serving and accomplishing a specific purpose. *God knows how to adjust the system, so that it brings Him the complete glory that He deserves*! For us as the people of God to declare that man has nothing to do with the Glory of God coming to our church houses is mere ignorance on our part. Man does have a role in the implementation of God's glory in the midst of His people. Not until Moses set everything in place and order in the natural did the Glory of God fill the Tabernacle. We are responsible to set the natural things in their proper place. That is the only way the Glory of God will operate in this Millennium Church.

God will orchestrate that which man cannot implement nor alter, so that He can make sure that man does not receive the Glory for all that He is doing in His Church. God will not share His Glory with flesh! God will open doors that no man can shut. At the same time, He will shut many doors that no man can open, and I must add, they will never be opened again! God just might step in to your church service next Sunday and say, "We interrupt this program to bring you a special news bulletin....I am taking over!"

He created the Garden of Eden and placed Adam and Eve over it and gave them dominion.

He set it in order, gave them the rules as to what was and was not allowed. Then God trusted them to abide by His system, not their own. The initial failure of man introduced the world to sin and short-circuited the system of our Creator. Yet He was not in any way defeated, but immediately stepped in and brought redemption to His initial plan which He had set in place.

Unfortunately, this failure produced a decrease in blessing. Had Adam and Eve operated by the laws of God, their blessings would have been of untold magnitude and increasing abundance. But because they forfeited God's system, methods, and plans the cost was tremendous. God's methods, plans, and processes do not need alteration. It is the methods, plans, and processes of mankind that need to be altered. *We should remember that God has a patent upon His creation and His Church. His Church is a unique design.* We can get into a lot of trouble when we put forth efforts to change what God has copyrighted in the heavens! If we will just allow God to operate His Church on His terms, we will see a mighty move in these days. We have no choice but to make Him the Head of the church, as the Scriptures command us.

As an *Organism*, we operate with a completely different mindset. We offer acceptance to God's schemes and plans, and we can operate with more liberality. We become thriving living creatures, that are not only products of life, but also we have ability through the power of the Spirit to produce life. We die to our way of doing things, and we are totally sold out to what God wants to do in and through us. *As an organization, God breathes upon us. As an organism, God breathes through us.* As an *organization*, we see the *heart* of God; as an *organism,* we hear and feel the *heartbeat* of God.

When the church allows herself to become a living, breathing organism, we see through the *eyes* of God. We have *ears to hear* what the Spirit has to say to the church. Our *hands* become God's Hands extended. Our *shoulders* are broadened and expanded to such magnitude We lack understanding as to how we can function in such a degree of success and carry the load at the same time. Our *arms* are *outstretched* so that we are willing to go to great lengths to reach the unlovable, to hold tightly to the hurting with every effort, to pour in the oil and to bring forth healing. At the drawing of His spirit and the sound of His voice, our *knees* will *bend* without hesitation; and we will unashamedly bow in the presence of a God who is an all consuming fire and stubbornly remain there until He burns out the dross in our lives.

In this place, He produces within us a desire to burn brightly for His Glory; and finally, the Millennium Church Body will have beautiful feet, *"How lovely on the mountains are the feet of them that spread good news..." (Nahum 1:15-Spirit Filled Life Bible).* The Church of The New Millennium will understand that we are all, according to our gifts and callings, ministers of the gospel; and our responsibility is to spread good news as well, not just the pastor and leadership. This type of mindset will catapult us into a new spiritual dimension and bring about the acceleration of the reaping of the Harvest! The Millennium Church will be the last day people that will make great harvest happen!

CHAPTER 2

The Model Church

Isaiah 60:1a "Arise, Shine, for thy light is come…"
(Spirit Filled Life Bible)

"The Millennium Church will not be motivated by doctrine not manipulated by tradition.. She will function AND succeed on scriptural principles found in the Word of the Living God."

Isaiah writes to us in Chapter 60, giving us a description of the future glory of the church. Much of the prophecies of this chapter have been taking place ever since Jesus was born and came to earth. He was sent by the Father to bring light to the Gentiles and that has been happening for thousands of years. The New Testament anointed ministry of Jesus set this chapter in Isaiah in motion, especially when He said to His disciples, "Go ye into all the world and preach the Gospel…." From that very moment in the life and ministry of Jesus, the prophecies of this chapter are being fulfilled over and over again.

There has always been a tremendous acceptance of the Word of God around the world. In foreign nations there is a hunger for God that is very evident. Preaching a salvation message across the ocean and thousands of people being born into the kingdom of God is not a difficult task. Such has not been the case in the United States of America. I am in no way insinuating that there has not been a work of the Holy Spirit in the United States. I am simply stating that the acceptance to the Gospel of Jesus Christ has been hard to come by. All of that is about to change and we are about to see this Nation turn to God in a very powerful way.

For many years, intercessors have prayed and sought God for an outpouring of revival in the United States. We have seen and heard of many outbreaks of people experiencing God in the Toronto Blessing, the Brownsville Revival, the Missouri Outpouring, and I am sure there are many others. As wonderful and powerful as these have been, they do not hold a candle to what we are about to see and experience, even in the local church fellowships! We are about to experience a real shaking in the Body of Christ. A radical revolution is about to take place throughout the church world! Old things are passing away and all things are becoming new.

Church Arising!

Why are we about to see revival come forth? Because, there is a new type of Church that is *arising*. She is known as "The Millennium Church." She will be a replica of the New Testament Church. She is coming up the backstretch and headed for the finish line taking everyone with her that will run alongside. This church is turning no one away from its doors. It is operating upon the Biblical concept that 'whosoever will, may come.' It has reserved seats for the poor as well as the rich.

Those two are gifted and those who will do nothing more than occupy a seat are welcome. The demon-possessed, the prostitute, the drug addict, the alcoholic, the gang leader, are obtaining occupancy in the front rows of our sanctuaries. Their lives are being changed by the Blood of Jesus and the power of the Gospel intrigues them as they experience the life changing application of the foolishness of the preaching of the Cross of Jesus Christ!

The word Arise comes from a Hebrew word known as QUM which means to rise up, establish, and strengthen. The New Millennium Church is arising from many areas as well as *in* many areas. This new church that is on the horizon will be very adamant about old things passing and all things becoming new. Its members will have no problem shedding grave clothes and rising up in the Power of the Holy Spirit to achieve their visions and accomplish their goals. They are challenged by the *Status-Quo*, and are termed miserable if they are not found about their Father's business.

The Millennium Church will have a corporate anointing to be a 'Change Agent'. We have seen this much in the past through various individuals, but seldom do we see it as a corporate function. Because of the focus upon unity, this Millennium Church will have the spiritual strength and stamina to literally take cities for the Glory of God. *Unity* will be their motto and *Unique* will be their theme. They will be daring and unafraid. They will not just be labeled as *Super Churches*, but they will be *Superlative Churches*. According to Daniel 11:32, they will know their God and do great exploits. They are arising from their places of complacency, drowsiness, and unfaithfulness. The words *apostasy* and *apathy* are not in their vocabulary, and these people who will make up this special church will have no understanding of their meanings. Their ongoing relationship with the Lord will increase their vision. This vision will be made plain to them upon the tables of their hearts, and they will run with it!

They will have new Biblical doctrines and traditions, fresh vision, fresh fire in their bones, and they will *rise* above the typical church body. There will be sounds that will crescendo from these Millennium Church Houses that have no other choice but to draw the attention of the societies which they are serving. People will come just to hear the sounds of prayer and intercession. Their ears will crave the sounds of the praise and worship. The Word of God will go forth in the power and demonstration of the Holy Spirit. God will move right in and make Himself at home, because The Millennium Church will be conducive to His very character.

The interior membership will be composed of *Achievers and Dreamers* that are willing to take a chance and try new things that have never been done in the church before. The Spiritual temperatures in these churches will be so fervent, that anything that is unrighteous or unlike God will not be able to exist. The hypocrites will not be able to survive in such an atmosphere.

They will have to run to the altar in repentance, or leave the premises.

Arising To Establish New Things

> *"I am a genuine believer that God desires to make His church houses Holy Habitations for Himself, not just places of Periodic Visitation….." (II Samuel 7:11- Leadership Bible, NIV)*

"The Lord declares to you that *'The Lord Himself'* will *establish* a house for you:

…I will raise up your offspring to succeed you, who will come from your own body, and I will *establish* his kingdom…" He is the one who will build a house for my Name, and I will *establish* his kingdom forever….

King David had a personal Prophet whose name was Nathan. In this passage of Scripture, Nathan received a powerful revelation from God regarding this awesome promise to bring *establishment* to David's family line forever. However, I believe we can make spiritual application to this as well. God's heart's desire in this hour is to establish for *Himself* a church that will glorify Him and Him alone! The average church house needs to look like the Lord *Himself,* and it should be a place where God *Himself* is comfortable. *I am a genuine believer that God desires to make His church houses holy habitations for Himself, not just places of periodic visitation.* The heart cry of God is to live and dwell among His own. He is not happy being a stranger in His own house, nor does it please Him when He feels like an intruder.

God also told Nathan that he would raise up David's offspring from his own body. As the Body of Christ, we must be willing to produce sons and daughters of the faith and release them into their ministry, calling and anointing in order for the harvest to be reaped. We cannot keep all membership within the walls of our churches that have a call of God upon their life and expect to see revival. We should respect the call upon their lives and send them out. *One major Biblical job description for the Pastor is to equip the saints for the work of the ministry.* Instead, in the past, we have been satisfied to keep them Biblically illiterate in order to keep them within our church walls. Pastors do that for many different reasons. Some are jealous of the gifts within their flock. Other pastors at times feel threatened by their calling. There are pastors and leadership who want to keep people there just for the sake of numbers. They do not want their attendance to fall because they do not want others to think they are not growing or that they have lost people.

When we as leaders release people into their gifts and send them out, we are not by any means losing. We can only gain. This is called the "RE-PRODUCTION" process. This is the key to reaping the harvest in the last days. Thirdly, God had already ordained that Solomon would build a house to glory *His Name*. God has already equipped and appointed those whom He desires to be the Apostles for these last day Millennium Churches. They are specially anointed ones. I am convinced that some of these Apostles, Prophets, Evangelists, and Pastor/Teachers are those that we are raising and equipping in our *OWN CHURCH BODIES*!

Webster defines the word '*Establish*' with at least three meanings, which I feel apply to this Millennium Church. The first one is "*To Be Recognized*." Recognition is something that almost everyone in church has had craving for, more so in the past rather than now. Instant gratification seems to be the state of expectancy for some, especially those of whom we know to be the 'Baby Boomer' crowd. If they are not bragged on, recognized continually, or lifted up in the limelight all of the time, then they are seemingly not interested in doing anything in the church. Colossians 3:17 exhorts us by saying, "And whatsoever you do in word or deed, do all in the Name of the Lord Jesus, giving thanks to God and the Father by Him." (Spirit Filled Life Bible) Yet, there is a place for recognition. Those whom you and I do not celebrate, we will lose. We must learn to distinguish between those who deserve the 'Law of Recognition', and those who have to receive a pat on the back for any and all efforts put forth by them.

For too many years, the church itself has been filled up with the 'Glory-Seekers'. These are people that have taken too much glory for themselves and have not given enough glory to God the Father for what is being done in the church. Any amount of Glory to man is TOO MUCH GLORY! The Millennium Church is bringing change to some of that. The folks who will make up this fellowship will be so in love with Jesus that they will have no desire to be recognized or even noticed. As long as they know that the Father sees, that is all that will matter to them.

The *Church* has always been recognized. She has consistently become a focal point in the eyes of people, whether it is for praise, approval or for criticism. I cannot say to you that criticism will cease, nor that praise and exaltation will increase. But I can say to you that if the church will be willing to decrease, that He will mightily increase. As long as Christ is seen in and through them, they will be at peace.

A New Mindset

They will eradicate from their fellowship the very mentality of 'We have not ever done it this way before!' They will bring into existence new programs that will teach and touch; new ideas that are not just "good ideas", but they will be definite "God ideas." GOD ideas will bring forth *Establishment and Existence in the Body.* No matter how much we try to implement, we must have gifted people who can bring *Establishment* to them. This is where the Church must begin to make room for the Prophet.

The Prophet will set in order, *establish, and stir up* necessary gifts, calling, and anointing that are either lying dormant, or have never been set in order before in the Kingdom of God. Fleshly or "Carnal" Doctrines; the Doctrines of men that are simply man's convictions and not at all Scripturally based, will have to be eradicated from our theological and philosophical brains.

Please take note that I said "fleshly doctrine." I am a firm believer in doctrine. Every church and denomination needs one, as long as it is *Biblical.* If the doctrines and traditions of men are set in place according to the Word of God, then people in general do not seem to have a problem with authority. When people are never heard and never responded to positively and their gifts and anointing are not recognized, they rise in rebellion. Prov. 29:2 says, "When the righteous are in authority, the people rejoice; but when a wicked man rules, the people groan." (Leadership Bible, NIV). We must remember that the church was built out of 'teamwork'. There is no 'I' in the word team. We are all in this together and we need each other. Once we learn this principle in the Body of Christ, I am convinced that we will see a greater settling among the people of God. We must learn to operate and flow out of relationship and not *just because* we have an authority figure over us.

We need authority, but it must be Godly authority. We read in Hebrews 13:17, "Obey them that have the rule over you, and submit yourselves: for they watch for your souls as they must give in account, that they may do it with joy, and not with grief: for that is unprofitable for you." (Leadership Bible, NIV; Full Life Study Bible).

This is by no means a statement made to create debatable issues regarding *theocracy or democracy*. The Church has had enough debates through the years and has suffered extreme repercussions because of them. Some have the belief that the church is a democracy and some insist that she is a theocracy. Personally, I believe that the Church is a combination of both. If we say that we are completely democratic, we are saying that the people are the governing force. To be totally theocratic is saying that only officials have a say so. By making such declarations, we have fully *rescued* ourselves from ever having to really work together in the church world; and therefore, we have committed *soul robbery*, having stolen from ourselves the privilege of serving one another out of *relationship*.

The Apostle Paul gives us a prime example of such relationship in the Book of Philemon. After Onesimus robbed Philemon and left him high and dry, Paul had opportunity to help him. While under house arrest in Rome, Onesimus visited Paul and he took advantage of the opportunity to disciple him. He later wrote a letter to Philemon requesting restoration of their *relationship*. In the book of Philemon verse 8, as he began to make his plea to Philemon on behalf of this now redeemed, runaway slave, he said: "Therefore, although in Christ I could be bold and *Order* you to do what you ought to do, yet I appeal to you on the basis of love...." (Leadership Bible, NIV).

In essence what Paul was saying to Philemon was that because of his position and authority, he actually had the power to command him to receive Onesimus back. However, because of their *'relationship In The Lord, and with one another'*, he felt that if he shared his heart with Philemon, he would respond as well because of his love and respect for Paul. Paul could have pushed his authority, forcing Philemon to accept Onesimus back, but he operated in love, out of *relationship*.

Sure, we must have leadership; but why not servant leadership. Before there can be effective *leadership*, we must have effective *relationship* one with another. How about a *"Towel Around The Waist Mentality?"* Jesus said to His disciples, "I have not come to be ministered unto, but to minister."(Spirit Filled Life Bible). Jesus was wreathed with servant-hood throughout His entire ministry upon the earth. At the close of the last supper with His disciples, Jesus stood up and took a towel from around His waist and began to wash their feet. Do we have pastors who are willing to wash the feet of their church members and leadership? Do we have church members and leaders who are willing to do the same for their pastor?

Leaders are served better if they move beyond formal, positional relationships with their followers. After all, is that not what we are praying and looking for? When we walk in servant leadership, we can eliminate a measure of *rebellion* that some followers may walk in. Paul was only able to help Philemon and Onesimus in this time of crisis because he had built a relationship with them both in the past. The Millennium Church will focus on serving and accomplishing through the building of relationships within the Body. There must be a new establishment of the importance of *servant leadership* and working together out of *relationship* within the Body of Christ. This church on the *rise* will be one that has no problem with establishment in the Kingdom of God. She will set in order and bring into existence a fresh mentality of Jesus Christ: "Servant-Leader Relationship."

Arising to Strengthen

Isaiah 35:3 "Strengthen ye the weak hands, and confirm the feeble knees…." (Full Life Study Bible, KJV)

Thirdly, The Millennium Church will be very instrumental in bringing strength to the people of God. There are some very weary saints within the walls of our churches. Those who have worked hard at building the church for many years are suffering from burn out; there are also those who are frustrated with things as they are and nothing seems to be in operation to bring about change. As I walk into various churches to minister, many times I can detect immediately the stench of discouragement among the people. There are many with the attitude that says, "Well, I have done this job for 20 years and I'm tired. Let somebody else do it now!" This Millennium Church needs to be keen enough in the elements of restoration that it will make every effort to bring healing to the people that are in that category.

Then, there will be those young Christians who have never really gotten their feet off of the ground with the Lord. In the process of their walk, they have become very weary and frustrated in trying to serve God. We as the people of God have an awesome responsibility to 'strengthen these weak hands, and to confirm these feeble knees.'

No More Spiritual Junk Food

Also, a new caliber of pastors and leadership must come forth for This Millennium Church. The old traditional ways of doing things just will not suffice in these last days. We must have a breath of fresh air. It is imperative that we have fresh bread from the pulpit. Manna that is stored up eventually begins to have a stench or odor. Teaching sessions that are carried on in our fellowships such as Sunday School, Bible studies, Children's Church, Teen Meetings, must be recognized as the "pure" Word of God. We must learn how to rightly divide the Word of God with wisdom and with zeal! As leaders and pastors we have fed our congregations far too much spiritual junk food. Just throwing something together on Saturday night at the midnight hour to feed our congregations on Sunday morning is not going to be sufficient any longer.

Hurting people that need to be strengthened are craving the Word of God with power. The apostle Paul declares, "I came not to you with enticing words of man's wisdom but in the power and demonstration of the Holy Ghost." (Leadership Bible, NIV). In the midst of their marital problems, they are not concerned with who the twelve tribes of Israel are. When their finances are in trouble, they could care less 'Who begot who'! We must begin to deliver messages from our pulpits that are relevant to the needs of people that we are serving and leading. Otherwise, we will not be able to retain them in our fellowships today.

When people walk into your fellowship, which is a good sign that they are hungry. Just remember, hungry people are easy to feed. Even if they are not hungry, there is always the possibility of making them hungry. All they have to do is smell something good and their desire to eat will take over. The aroma of fresh bread will stir up an appetite, creating hunger.

As pastors and leaders in the church today, we must realize that our congregations are not filled with uneducated people any longer. They are well trained, educated individuals who are looking for spiritual leadership that have knowledge of the Word of God. Teaching and preaching the word of God without anointing will not satisfy the spiritual hunger in the lives of today's society. People are looking for the sincere milk of the Word as well as the meat of the Word! We have to produce both. You have heard it said that 'You can lead a horse to water, but you cannot make him drink'. I believe that is true. However, I also believe that if you make him thirsty enough, you do not have to make him drink! The fresh bread of Heaven, the Word of God, and clear brisk water from the river of God will produce spiritual stamina in the individual Christian therefore producing a strong healthy body! We must do whatever necessary to strengthen the hearts of people.

The Word of God will build up spiritual muscles and cause us to take on a new form as children of God. "Faith cometh by hearing, and hearing by the Word of God." The Word teaches us how to stand on our own two feet spiritually. If you take a man that is hungry and cook him a fish, he will eat that fish and eventually he will become hungry again. However, if you teach HIM how to cook that fish, he will never be hungry again.

I Thessalonians 3:13 declares to us "May He strengthen your hearts so that you will be blameless and holy in the presence of our God and Father when our Lord Jesus comes with all His holy ones." (Full Life Study Bible, KJV) I openly declare to you prophetically, that I believe that The Millennium Church will be Mrs. Personality! It will be a place where God will show up and He will show out! He will show Himself powerful!

She will be a group exhibiting the Glory of the Lord that we will experience before the Second Coming of Christ. We need to pour into our congregations all that is necessary in order to strengthen them for this final hour. The heart of the Body of Christ must be strengthened. Several years ago, in a time of intercession the Lord gave me a prophetic word for His body. I know that it was a futuristic word.

"In the days to come says the Lord of Hosts, I will cause a new flow of my blood throughout my body. New arteries will be opened and I will strengthen the valves of my heart says the Lord. Where there have been blockages in the Spirit, I will do spiritual bypasses and open-heart surgery to produce new energy in my people. In some I will do a heart transplant removing the stony heart and replacing with a heart of flesh. This freedom of my blood flow will strengthen my people and produce new energy to build my body says the Lord of Hosts."

We are living in a time of fear and uncertainty. God is raising up The Millennium Church to lift up the hands that are weak, to confirm the feeble knees, and to strengthen the hearts of those who remain. We need to teach them from the Word of God how to apply fresh applications of grace for each new day. This church that I am speaking to you about is rising up in strength, so that she can strengthen others, as she needs to. God is calling us to be *recognizable* as His children in these final hours. We must *establish* some new things in His Name. The church must arise in strength so that she can *strengthen* those things, which remain.

CHAPTER 3

The Maternal Church

Isaiah 60:1b "And the Glory of the Lord has risen upon thee....."(Leadership Bible, NIV)

Whenever folks say to me "I heard you *planted a church*," I say to them, "No, I *birthed a church.*"

Having grown up in the church, I have been made aware of the tremendous emphasis that has been put upon the importance of the "church" as a whole. I believe in order to reach the harvest in this last day; we must produce more and more churches. The term 'church planting' has been used over and over again in the church world. I have tremendous respect for those who have pioneered churches in their lifetime. One reason for that is because I myself have pioneered a church and was the pastor of that church for seven years. *When folks say to me, "I heard that you planted a church," I say, "No, I gave birth to a church!"* If you will allow me in these next few pages, I would like to present to you, what I believe to be, a revelatory concept that God gave to me in the process of starting my church.

Worship

I believe that there are at least five necessary stages that we must go through in order to give birth to a vision. The first one is called *worship*.

In Luke 1, we read where the Angel Gabriel appeared to Mary in the city of Nazareth and said to her, "Hail, thou art highly favored; the Lord is with thee: Blessed art thou among women….."(Spirit Filled Life Bible).

First of all, we should make note that in the Word of God, angels were often used as representatives of God Himself, therefore imputing the presence of God with an atmosphere of worship whenever and wherever they may have appeared. In Isaiah Chapter six, the Seraphim's, or the 'Burning Ones', were flying in the temple saying, "Holy, Holy, Holy, is the Lord God Almighty; the whole earth is full of His Glory."(Leadership Bible, NIV). They were simply setting the stage for the call from God to Isaiah to preach the Gospel to the world. In this story of Mary's divine conception, Gabriel had been employed by God to set forth an atmosphere of *worship*, so that Mary would accept the message that he was assigned to bring to her that night.

In an atmosphere of Worship we not only hear from God, but as revelation takes place, we have the opportunity to respond to Him.

God also gave her more than just another *opportunity* to respond, but also the *option* to respond to Him in worship. Gabriel made three profound proclamations to her right in the midst of a *worship* atmosphere. First of all, he said to her "Hail, thou art highly favored…."

God was about to give Mary the opportunity to do something that would require tremendous *grace* upon her. So He sent Gabriel to assure her that she was special in His eyes.

He was granting her a God-given ability to believe in herself and be totally dependent upon Him for the task before her. This impartation of grace will enable us from time to time to accomplish those things, which we know we are unable to do within ourselves. To carry out and fulfill the call of God upon our lives requires a certain amount of self-confidence. We must feel good about ourselves and our relationship with the Lord in order to be successful. Grace that is functional and operative within us reveals the magnitude of a spiritual dimension that says, "....It is not by might, nor by power, but it is by my Spirit says the Lord!"(Zechariah 4:6-Leadership Bible, NIV).

It literally takes on the form of our need, becomes everything to us in our time of testing and trial, and as grace unfolds before us, enables us to receive from the hand of God. Mary was going to experience the unfolding grace and favor of God. How can we explain the word 'Grace'? Grace is a substance that will manifest itself in the form of spiritual energy that flows from the risen Savior. It will strengthen us to succeed in the accomplishment of His divine will simply by the indwelling of the Holy Spirit in us. Grace becomes a support mechanism for the soul when we are experiencing spiritual weakness. It helps us to understand that it is in Him that we live, and move, and have our being! Grace is a force as well as favor!

The Millennium Church will be graced with the *favor of God*! *They will be impregnated with the ability to accomplish in the Spirit those things, which others have tried to accomplish for years through the flesh!*

The second thing the angel Gabriel said to her was "...the Lord is with thee..." Just the very assurance that the Lord is with us is sometimes all that is required for the called of God to pursue Him in worship. Once we pursue Him in worship, He will then reveal His purposes for us. I am not saying that we must always wait on a feeling in order to worship. I am simply stating that worship is something we do, knowing that God is there whether we feel Him or not! With the tasks ahead of her, Mary would need to know in her heart that even in the times when God would be silent that He would never be still. She needed to know that God would always be working to bring about His Glory in her and through her.

The same principle applies to The Millennium Church. She will know that the Lord is with her and that nothing shall be impossible with God!!! This caliber of church will walk in levels of faith that will rock the world of the traditional church. The power of God will be the ordinary setting instead of something that just happens out of the ordinary. Those who know that the Lord is with them will be chosen to do tremendous tasks in the Kingdom of God. Everlasting joy will be upon the heads of those who make up the congregations of these Millennium Churches.

It will be mandatory that we walk in assurance in all that we do that the Lord is with us.

The tasks put before us as a church body in this day, will require both blessing and suffering; joy and sadness; successes and some disappointments. However, despite the opposition from the outside world, we will go forth and pursue, knowing that the Lord is with us and that we are more than conquerors through Him who loved us and gave Himself for us. Tasks God puts before us will never be greater than the Power behind us.

The Apostle Paul said it like this in Philippians 3:10 & 11. "That I may know Him in the power of His resurrection, and the fellowship of His sufferings, being made conformable to His death; If by any means, I might attain unto the resurrection of the dead."(Spirit Filled Life Bible). He is simply saying that his desire is to serve Christ, no matter what the cost! The New Millennium Church will have the same attitude.

She will express her heart for God by pursuing Him in a more intimate relationship than most church bodies. This pursuit will consist of persistence in the spirit man to know the Lord on a more personal level. The members will hunger and pant after the heart of God and therefore will be well versed in His Word. His nature, character, and ways will lace their very lives on a daily basis. This church will have a desire to listen to His Word and respond in faith and obedience.

To desire to know Him in the power of His resurrection will produce in these people renewal of life, healing, miracles, and their own personal resurrection from the dead. They will be willing to share in His sufferings by personal denial, by daily crucifixion of the flesh, and simply by suffering for His sake. The very fact that "...the Lord is with thee...." will be reflected in the lifestyle of this church!

Then thirdly, Gabriel said to Mary, "....Blessed art thou among women...." Have you ever noticed the glow on the countenance of a pregnant woman? There is radiance upon her face that is comparable to none. I believe that is because the creation of God is growing within her, and she has been chosen by God for the task of birthing a child, God's own creation. She knows that she is about to grow and produce a product of an intimate love relationship that will bring her joy for many years to come. There is a masterpiece that is growing and developing within her womb that is fearfully and wonderfully made by the hand of our Father. I believe that this is comparably true with the church. She should radiate with the countenance of His Glory! For from the church should come forth many, many children for the Kingdom of God.

I have always depicted the church in my own heart as a spiritual womb that would become impregnated with a vision conceived by the Holy Ghost. When Jesus looks at His church, he should be able to say, "Blessed art thou among women." Even as Gabriel recited these words to her, she did not understand what exactly he was saying. In fact the Scriptures tell us that she was troubled at his saying and that she was trying to 'figure out' what kind of greeting this was. She must have been wondering what in the world Gabriel was talking about?

Whenever we are called by God for a particular assignment, one of the spirits of the underworld called *fear* will seemingly try to grasp hold of us. It sometimes will make an unwelcome entrance and say, "Excuse me, may I say a word?" If we allow fear to speak, which it does have the ability to do, at that point we will begin to see our own inadequacies. Fear of failure will set in; and if we are not cautious, we will find ourselves in a prison of spiritual recession and never become all that God desires us to be.

God was asking Mary to become not just the mother of the Savior of the World, but of the Foundation of the church!

As Gabriel beheld her countenance, laced with a spirit of fear and uncertainty, he immediately responded with the first promise that he gave her, "Mary do not be afraid; thou art highly favored." The Millennium Church will be like a 'Church of Churches!'

There will be episodes of fear and uncertainty; there will be those times of risk taking. There will be those times of wondering if what we are hearing from the Lord is REALLY from the Lord!

Gabriel was reassuring Mary that she was not only favored, but that she was highly favored! The tasks ahead of the church today are indeed great. However, we cannot pull back from this last opportunity that God is giving us as a people. The church is the offspring of Jesus Christ. God was not only asking Mary to just give birth to the savior, but also to the foundation of the church. The church is built upon Jesus Christ the solid rock! She is the greatest enterprise that exists in the earth today. Isaiah prophesied that of the "Increase of His Government there shall be no end." The foundation of this enterprise that was about to come forth from the *WOMB* of Mary was set to change the spiritual course of the whole earth!

Conception

Luke 1:31 – "And, behold, you shall conceive in your womb, and bring forth a son, and shall call his name JESUS."(Leadership Bible, NIV)

The second stage of birthing a vision is called *'conception'*. It is in those intimate times of *worship* that visions are *conceived*. That is when the wombs of our hearts become fertile, and we become one with the will and the plan of the Holy Spirit. Those fiery passionate times of intercession are the breeding ground for us to become impregnated with the purpose and the plan of God, both for us and for the church. From the very moment of conception, life begins. In these days, God will begin to raise up those with the spirit of the pioneer that will have passion and desire to give birth to the New Millennium Church! These men and women must be called by God, not parents, grandparents, pastors, and Sunday school teachers to name a few.

One of the definitions of Webster for the word conceive, is '*…to be founded or formed in a certain way….*' The only way that conception can happen in the natural is for there to be a physical *union* between male and female. The same is true with the church in a spiritual sense. The Holy Spirit and the spirit of man must become united in order for conception to happen. The only opportunity for *conception in the Spirit* is in the time of *intimacy with the Father.* In and from the time of conception, there are some very unique things that take place. Formation is set in order. Can you imagine how many problems could be prevented in the Body of Christ if only we would spend intimate time with Him and receive His plan of *formation* for His Body?

Instead, we just operate from our own initiative and structure something that does not even come near to resembling our Heavenly Father. Churches that are formed by the hand of flesh always have to deal with the flesh within them. Before we start churches, we need to make sure that our motivation is right and that we are doing it for the right reasons. Therefore, we could save ourselves much conflict. Of course, we will always have to deal with problems within the church. *When we are in the people business we are in the problem business. The more sheep that we have, the more mess we have to clean up!* Problems are solved easier when we operate out of the Spirit instead of the flesh.

Another meaning of the word conception is *"design".* The Psalmist David declares to us in Psalm 139:13 & 14, *"For thou hast possessed my reins: thou hast covered me in my mother's womb. I will praise thee; for I am fearfully and wonderfully made."*(Leadership Bible, NIV). God is creatively and actively involved in the development of human life. He personally cares for a baby from the moment of its conception. God has a special design for each individual. No two people are exactly alike. Even with multiple births, there is a difference somewhere. The same is true with the church. All churches are different in some way. They have diverse personalities; they operate differently from other churches. Architectural structures almost always differ, and the interior functions of the church are usually not the same as others.

God covers every child in the mother's womb. *During the visitation of the angel to Mary, he informed her that the Holy Ghost would come upon her and the power of the Highest would overshadow her.* He was covering the foundation of the church in the womb of His mother! We are all God's own unique design, The church is the same way. We are fearfully and wonderfully made by the touch of the Master. Just as individuals, Churches should be the masterpiece of God!

The Millennium Church must bring forth children that resemble Jesus Christ. The church must look, walk, and talk like Jesus. They should most definitely love like Him and carry His fragrance everywhere they go. As Mary anointed the feet of Jesus with such fragrant, costly perfume, she was fragranced by Him as she touched Him. From that point on in her life, everywhere that Mary went, the Lamb was sure to go! His personality, character, and fragrance should precede us in all of our Christian efforts. He desires to be the center of attention and the main attraction in our church gatherings. We must be bathed in love and compassion for others and win the lost to Christ at any cost. We must be like those who are willing to bear His name and not be ashamed.

A third meaning of the word conceive, is *"plan."* Jeremiah 29:11 tells us "For I know the thoughts that I think towards you, says the Lord, thoughts of peace and not of evil, to give you an unexpected end."(Leadership Bible, NIV). God has a plan for every life, even from the womb. God said to Jeremiah, "Before I formed thee in the belly, I knew thee, and before thou camest forth out of the womb, I sanctified thee, and I ordained thee a prophet to the nations." Please note the comparison with Luke 1:31. "And behold, thou shalt conceive in thy womb, and bring forth a son, and shall call His Name Jesus!" Verse 35 says, "Therefore also that holy thing which shall be born of thee shall be called the Son of God!"(Leadership Bible, NIV).

God has a plan for everyone in this universe. The Millennium Church also has a plan in store for her that only the hand of God can design. This Millennium Church has a destiny. A destiny that is set in place, designed, ordered, and planned by the Master Creator. The word destiny means, 'an unusually inevitable course of events.' Doesn't this describe this Millennium Church that I have been talking to you about? This church is so different that the onlooker will know and recognize that God's plans are not our plans and God's thoughts are not our thoughts!

Doesn't it make us realize that God has a plan for us, to give us a future and a hope! What a blessed promise.

Mary had to rise above intimidation in order to fulfill her destiny that God was laying before her. She was going to have to be determined to turn a deaf ear to the critic and to opinionated people in order to fulfill her call. The church has a destiny. She is destined to rule and reign with Christ forever. This Millennium Church must also, regardless of who or what, conceive the vision and the plan of God and move forward for the sake of the call. We must become impregnated with vision that will fully reveal to us that JESUS is the foundation of This Millennium Church. In Corinthians 3:11 declares, "For no other foundation can no man lay than that is laid, which is Jesus Christ."(Spirit Filled Life Bible). It is upon Him that we must build. He himself said to Peter, "…Upon this Rock, I will build my Church…." Jesus must be at the center of The Millennium Church! And we must learn to build upon the Rock that never fails.

Gestation

Luke 1:32 – "He shall be great, and shall be called the Son of the Highest…"(Leadership Bible, NIV).

Third phase of a Church Vision is called *gestation*. Gestation means "to carry in the womb from the very moment of conception up to the delivery." Gestation is simply the growth process of the fetus. Once conception takes place, then the growth should start. The Millennium Church will be a type church that will grow forth strong, powerful people. These people, who mature and grow spiritually, will be those people who will endure to the end. Growth is a process. It does not happen overnight. It takes time. The extent of this process will produce not only growth, but patience and long-suffering. One definition of growth is *'expansion'*. Expansion means "to swell or enlarge." It seems to me that the primary focus of churches today is to grow numerically. If we could only realize that the spiritual growth must precede numerical growth. As Gabriel said to Mary that her Son would be *'GREAT'*, He was saying He shall become large, and expanded, (there are many more definitions of this word 'great').

Sure, we know that His ministry reached the entire world. He came into the world as an International Savior. I believe that He was talking about much more than geographical territory. Luke 2:52 states *"And Jesus increased in wisdom and stature, and in favor with God and man."*(Leadership Bible, NIV). This New Millennium Church will have a desire to increase in stature and wisdom in order to please the Father. The scriptures tell us that as Jesus submitted to his mother and father and returned home with them, *'He increased'*. In order for Jesus' ministry to expand geographically, it was imperative that He increase with and in God. Jesus was 30 years of age before His ministry was launched forth. Why? One of the reasons was preparation. As Jesus submitted to His spiritual authority, in the following eighteen years, He would be prepared for *expansion* in a world-wide ministry.

When we operate in humility that is the atmosphere in which we become exalted in the Lord. We have to be willing to go through the process, or the proper channels in order for healthy growth to come. Our churches in the past have been saturated with multiplied immaturity. *Growth requires stretching.* As we become impregnated with *vision,* stretching is inevitable.

In a human pregnancy, as the baby grows, and the womb enlarges and expands, the body stretches and things move around in order to make room for the growth and development of the fetus. Immaturity in heart and mind can stunt the growth of both our personal being and the church as well. We must be willing to give way to things that we have never done before in the Body of Christ. We must be teachable. Jesus was teachable or else He would not have gone home with His parents that day after teaching the doctors and lawyers.

Even though they were astounded at His teachings, He, as well as Mary and Joseph, his earthly parents knew that He had much more to learn. This New Millennium Church will have a desire to increase in stature and wisdom, and she must have the desire in order to *increase* at all in other areas. For instance, the Apostle Paul says in Ephesians 4:14a-15, "That we henceforth be no more children…. (15) But speaking the truth in love, may grow up into Him in all things, which is the head, even Christ."(Leadership Bible, NIV). To be spiritually mature means to be able to speak the truth in love and not to act like children in the process. II Peter 3:18 exhorts us to "Grow in the grace and the knowledge of our Lord and Savior, Jesus Christ."(Leadership Bible, NIV). Growth in spiritual things must happen for The Millennium Church. Paul said to the Corinthian people, "When I was a child, I thought as a child, I spoke as a child, but when I became a man, I put away childish things…" That is maturity and growth.

Development is not the same thing as growth. Many churches believe that because they have new thoughts, ideas, programs etc…. that exhibits growth. Such is not the case. You can have growth without development. We see that in children who are born with handicaps. They have been growing, but they have not had healthy development. Deformities set in during the growth process, and they create physical difficulties. Many times the child is harmed for life. Disabilities have to be dealt with on a daily basis. This is a clear picture of some of the more traditional churches of the past. They experience growth, but not development.

We sometimes try to grow before we start to develop. We need to learn that much of this process must take place at the same time. If we want to grow our churches, we must grow spiritually ourselves first. Otherwise, as new people come to our fellowships and accept Christ, we will not be equipped to help them grow and develop. Lambs do not feed lambs. Sheep feed lambs! We must grow and develop first in order to help others grow and develop. If not, the following will happen. Hosea 9:11-14 says, "As for Ephraim, their glory will fly away like a bird, from the birth, and from the womb, and from the conception….though they bring up their children, I will bereave them, …Give them, Oh Lord: what will thou give? Give them a miscarrying womb and dry breasts." (Spirit Filled Life Bible).

The Millennium Church will be dedicated to give this last day harvest the necessary elements for its positive and powerful growth. If we are growing, then we can help others grow. Otherwise, we are simply allowing them to die twice. New converts will hunger in these last days, and they will grow quickly. However, if we are not prepared to feed them and nurture them along the way, their glory will fly away like a bird, from the *BIRTH*, and from the *WOMB*, and from the *CONCEPTION*! All the groundwork that we have laid will be lost, even from the conception of the burden.

The churches that are not increasing in wisdom and stature will become miscarrying wombs and abort those who are not developing; or the Lord will give dry breasts; and because they are not being properly fed, they will wilt and die spiritually. The New Millennium Church will not allow this to happen in the Body of Christ. She will have a *Maternal Instinct* that will cause her to take care of her children and see them grow and develop at a healthy rate. He shall be great and shall be called the Son of the Highest….To become great will require a growth process in us first. We must *Become* in order to *Expand*! The Millennium Church shall be great, and shall be called the Son of the highest, as gestation takes place in her womb. Luke 1:35 "And the angel answered and said unto her, The Holy Ghost shall come upon thee, and the power of the Highest shall overshadow thee…." (Leadership Bible, NIV).

This simply tells us that there will be a covering of the Glory of the Lord as gestation takes place in the womb of His Bride. The angel also informed Mary that the thing which is growing within her womb "…is of the Holy Ghost!" This was a total work of God! It was performed in such a way that man could not take any glory for it at all. The same precedence is being laid for This Millennium Church. It will be so structured by the hand of God, breathed upon by the breath of God Himself; there will be no way that the world can deny that she is solely the creation of the Father. She will look just like Him. God will glorify her, that she may bring Him all the Glory that He deserves and has not received from others who claim to be "His Body."

Travail

Fourthly, *travail* is a vitally important element in the ministry of vision. Travail is an offspring of intercession. Travail releases the creative power or energy of the Holy Spirit into a situation to produce, to create, or to give birth to something. Now if I were to say to you that this type of Church was coming forth without pain, then I would certainly be telling you an untruth. There will be some pain involved. Webster defines the word travail as *suffering, distress, anguish, etc*...After the gestation process and the child is grown to full development, travail will be the next step in the maternal instinct process. There will have to be some pushing involved. The Word of God speaks to us in several areas about travail. Isaiah 66:7&8 says, "Before she travailed she brought forth; before her pain came, she brought forth a man child. Who hath heard such a thing? Who hath seen such things?....For as soon as Zion travailed, sons and daughters were born...." (Spirit Filled Life Bible).

The travail will be very intense in this last day church. Intercession will be the platform for the travailing, weeping, mourning, lamenting that will take place in The Body of Christ and will bring forth the birth. "For when Zion travails sons and daughters shall be born." Travail is in the only way to bring forth a birth. Birth does not happen before travail. She will not bring forth children until *travail* takes place. Travail is not a fun place to be. It is very painful Miserable describes it well, but not fully! I would like to bring to your attention several things regarding travail.

Travail is the most painful part of a pregnancy. That is the part that women dread the most about childbirth. It certainly requires something more powerful than a pat on the back, or someone noticing that you are screaming down the hospital corridor. As Gabriel was conversing with Mary one of the statements that came forth from him in Luke 1:31 was, "...and behold thou shalt conceive in the womb, *AND BRING FORTH A SON*..."(Leadership Bible, NIV). *Travail is the only avenue by which children can be brought forth.*

The same principal is true in The Word of God. Travail is a painful process. Something unique to me about this part of birth is the fact that no one else can do it for you...you must bring forth yourself. Others can help you pray, but they cannot give birth to anything unless they are impregnated with something. Even with the strongest medicines sometimes they just cannot ease the pain. The Millennium Churches are going to bring forth birth and they will do this quickly!

In Exodus Chapter 1, the King of Egypt gave instruction to the midwives regarding the babies of the Hebrew women. They helped them give birth to their babies. They actually had an assignment of adoption for a season of the child's young life. Ezekiel describes abandoned Jerusalem as being adopted by God. Ezekiel 16:4-7 "As for the day of your nativity, on the day you were born, your navel cord was not cut, nor were you washed in water to cleanse you; you were not rubbed with salt nor wrapped in swaddling clothes. No eye pitied you to do any of these things for you, to have compassion on you, but you were thrown out in the open field....I made you thrive like a plant in the field; and you grew, matured, and became very beautiful...." (Leadership Bible, NIV).

The tasks of the Hebrew women involved five different steps.

They were to coach the mother through her delivery. Instruction plays a large role in the success of The Millennium Churches. A new caliber of pastor/teacher will be released to minister in these churches in order to produce and reproduce healthy fetuses. These babies will need the sincere milk of The Word of God and a healthy diet as they develop and grow. They will not survive on spiritual 'Junk Food.' They must progress from the milk to the meat. They must be taught The Word of God and not 'preached at!' The reproduction process requires maturity. Lambs do not feed lambs; sheep feed lambs.

They were to cut the umbilical cord. Once the Birth process has been completed, then the child must be released to breathe, sleep and eat without total dependence upon his mother. Millennium Churches will produce independent children that will seek after knowledge and direction from The Holy Spirit without staying attached to the mother church forever with no survival on their own. Yet they will always have a watchful eye upon their young as they progress toward development and maturity. They will remain in position to bring them to safety if necessary.

They were to bathe the Baby. Maternal Churches will raise sanctified children through The Word of God. The Apostle Paul said we are washed and we are sanctified through The Word of God! Showers of blessing for These Millennium Churches are mandatory! These babies need to be bathed with The Water of Life, Jesus Christ Himself! Can you recall how refreshed you feel whenever you step out of a shower? You feel as if you can conquer the day!

There is not one place on the body that the water has not saturated! There is a feeling of cleanliness, and even a fragrance that is noticeable by others. To shower implies to saturate.

On the other hand, you can take a bath and what does it do? It relaxes you. It becomes a place of serenity. A private time of winding down, of rest, and of peace. There is a 'pouring on of the water' in bathing. Water is applied only in necessary places of the body. Both of these applications are healthy processes in the growth and development of the spiritual aspects of a child. There is strength and yet there is peace all from the same flow of the water of The Word of God. "To bathe" means to 'apply and saturate specific parts.' As the midwives ministered to the babies through bathing them, they were washing away impurities that they may have received while in the womb of their mother.

They were to rub the baby with salt in a belief that it promoted good health. Did not Jesus say, we are the salt of the earth? Salt is a healing agent that must be used again in this last day for the healing of His church. Salt is also a preservative. It causes foods to be preserved so that they do not go bad. How we need this preservative process in The Body of Christ today! They were to wrap them in snuggly swaddling clothes. They were instructed that as the Hebrew women gave birth they were to be killed immediately. The Bible declares to us that the midwives feared God instead of Pharaoh, and they saved all the male babies that they could. When the king heard what they had done, he began to deal with them. They responded by telling him in verse 19, that the Hebrew women were not as the Egyptian women. The Hebrew women were lively and they were having their babies before the midwives could ever get to them! The Hebrew women sat on what was called a 'birthing stool'. This was a simple, round stool, with a hole in the middle. As they would have their labor pains and push, the babies would drop through the holes in the stools and the midwives would take over from there.

That is how This Millennium Church will give birth to people. They will be quick. No time to waste! The travail must begin for the birth is about to come forth! This church will give birth to more babies by sitting on birthing stools than most traditional churches have ever done by sitting on pews! Why? Because *intercession* is the platform of *intimacy* where *conception* takes place. There will be a Holy Fire that burns within them that is called *zeal!* The word zeal means fervor, intensity, and excitement…zeal will produce *gestation* and gestation will bring on *travail*. They cannot wait to have these babies! Actually, they cannot have them fast enough! These churches will be lively churches!

In Galatians Chapter 4, and verse 19, the Apostle Paul gives us a little different insight to the word travail. He said, "My little children, of whom I *travail in birth* again until Christ be formed in you… ."(Leadership Bible, NIV). In this scripture, the word travail comes from a Greek word 'Odino' which means "the pains of childbirth." It expresses to us Paul's concern for these Galatian people who have become alienated from Christ and have fallen from Grace. Paul was filled with heartache, affliction, pain, and yearning. He is *travailing* for them because he felt that they needed a second spiritual birth. He takes on the birth pangs of a mother in order for Christ to be formed in them.

We may not fully understand all of the scriptural application of these verses but there is one thing for sure – The Holy Spirit is definitely in control. Travail has to do with spiritual reproduction, and maturity is shown forth in the process, and intensity is ever present in it.

The bowels of intercession and travail within the very fiber of This Millennium Church will not just see the unsaved accept Christ, but this Church will *maintain* such a revival atmosphere that they will see those who have left their first love return to Christ with joy.

All across Christendom, churches will have 24-hour prayer rooms, prayer chains, and emergency telephone lines for prayer. Those in The Body of Christ who feel the call or have the desire to pray will be both called to pray and drawn into intercession by The Holy Spirit in the last days.

Because of this type of prayer and intercession, backsliders will receive new strength to live for Jesus as they come back to Him in total repentance. The sick will be healed, marriages will be mended, folks will receive the Baptism of The Holy Spirit, people will be called to ministry, and all of these miracles will come about because of the willingness on the parts of individuals to pay the price of travail.

Birth

Luke 1:35 "Therefore that Holy thing which SHALL BE BORN OF THEE shall be called the Son of God."(Leadership Bible, NIV).

The fifth element in *birthing* a vision is the church itself coming forth. The Holy Spirit was coming upon Mary and the child would be conceived solely as a miraculous work of God. As a result of this, Jesus would be completely holy, and He would be a product of life which no man would have anything to do with, nor could take the credit for.

The Millennium Churches will reflect evidence that man has had very little to do with the progress of the church. God's glory will overshadow the church and the power of the Highest will rest upon her. *As travail sets in and the church begins to PUSH, then the birth of new things in the realm of The Spirit will come forth.*

Let me share with you several prophetic insights about The Birthing of This Millennium Church. First of all, I believe that we need to seek God for the specific towns and cities in which these churches are to come to birth. The reason for that is taken from Luke 2:15. *"So it was, when the angels had gone away from them into heaven, that the shepherds said one to another,' Let us now go unto BETHLEHEM and see this thing that has come to pass, which the Lord has make known unto us."(Spirit Filled Life Bible).*

The name *'Bethlehem'* means *'House Of Bread'*. I have already stated in the first chapter the vital importance of making sure that we feed the people of God fresh bread from Heaven. The caliber of people that God will send to our churches in these last days will be people that are hungry for the real Word of God. The very cities where we will conceive this caliber of church must be a place that will give forth the aroma of freshness. Ecclesiastes 10:1 declares, "Dead flies putrefy the perfumer's ointment, and cause it to give off a foul odor."(Leadership Bible, NIV). These Millennium Churches will not house foul odors. The very Breath of God will breathe upon His people as they gather for their times of worship. These churches being the ultimate work of The Holy Spirit will not have 'Houseatosis!'

There will be meat, and not just milk in these church houses! Jesus, The Bread of Life Himself will be the very focus of the congregations. Those things, which may be dead, will not be allowed to spoil the anointed fragrance of The Holy Spirit! There will be no unpleasant stench in these 'Houses Of Bread'. The cities where these churches are birthed must be analyzed and spiritually mapped in order to determine exactly where they need to be placed. The Names of Churches and their locations are of extreme importance.

Secondly in verse 16, "And they came with haste, and found Mary and Joseph, and the Babe lying in a manger." (Leadership Bible, NIV). There will be such anointing on The Millennium Churches that people will come with *haste* in order to find Jesus. There was significance to their coming so rapidly. These churches will move in an accelerated pace, such as never before. They will not be able to do enough, quickly enough. Pastors will not have to beg these congregations to come to church, or even work within the church. The desire will be inbred within them as they build healthy relationships with the Father, pursue the heart of The Father and see His kingdom come to earth as it is in Heaven!

These congregations will *bring forth* a caliber of church that will reveal the Glory of The Lord. Just as Mary *brought forth* her first born Son….So will these churches bring forth the Glory of God into their midst. They will operate in unity and the power of The Holy Spirit will be at work in their midst! What an awesome challenge for us to *bring forth* that, which will resemble the Son of God!

Then Thirdly, in verse 17, "And when they had seen *Him*, they made widely known the saying which was told them concerning this Child."(Leadership Bible, NIV). After the shepherds had seen Him for themselves, they began to spread the news that The Savior had been born. How we need churches to witness more and experience the zeal of spreading the gospel of Jesus Christ with fervor. These shepherds were not ashamed that they had met The Christ-child. They told everyone whom they could find! The Millennium Church will be a church that will *bring forth* salvation *through the proclamation of having seen Him for themselves!*

Where did they see Him? In the Church! Hallelujah! Just like the Prophet Isaiah, they will see Him high and lifted up and sitting upon His throne as His train fills the temple! As they behold The Lamb of God in their services and *worship* Him, conception will take place for the salvation of others, the burden will begin to *gestate*, they will begin to weep and *travail* over their souls, and they will *birth* or *bring forth new souls for The Kingdom of God!*

Fourthly, in verse 18, "and all those who heard it *marveled* at those things that were told them by the shepherds."(Leadership Bible, NIV). The beautiful thing to me about the birthing process is the fact that it is within itself, so miraculous, and actually beyond human explanation. As the shepherds shared what they had seen, heard, and experienced, then the people with whom they shared, *marveled.* There is just something about giving birth to Jesus in our churches, cities, and towns that seems to get the attention of those who are standing by. Millennium Churches will have no problem drawing people to their church because they have their priorities in the right order. They have come through the birth process and those onlookers will be ready to hear about this man called Jesus when this church is released to them. Just as the people were awaiting the Messiah, groping in darkness and grasping for hope, so are folks today sitting in churches dying by the scores for the birth of Jesus to come forth in a church, a city, or a town close to them.

Isaiah 66:9 asks the question "Shall I bring to the time of birth and not cause delivery?" Says The Lord. "Shall I who cause delivery, shut up the womb?" says your God. (Leadership Bible, NIV). It is imperative that we understand once the baby moves down into the birth canal; the only thing left to do is *PUSH!* Would God let us go through the intimacy of worship, then conception, gestation, travail, and then not give us the strength to bring forth the baby in our spiritual wombs? No, I do not think so. Otherwise, the baby would die in our birth canal. We have too many churches that have died in the birth canal of the mother church.

The Millennium Church will be that special *mother church,* who in love will do all that is necessary to bring forth the birth! Birthing requires pushing! Pushing in childbirth is not an easy task. It requires such things as strength, stamina, determination, coaching, excitement, and anticipation. However, the maternal instinct in each woman is to push that baby to new life.

No Birth Control!

Isaiah 66:9 "Shall I who cause delivery shut up the womb?" says the Lord. (Leadership Bible, NIV).

The New Millennium Churches will feel and see the need to give birth to daughter churches. They will birth them fast, even as the Hebrew women did on the birthing stools in Egypt! They will not believe in spiritual birth control! They will be fertile and produce daughter churches on a regular basis. As long as they are willing to produce, The Lord will not shut the womb!

From the time of conception, that baby is just a vision or a hope that will come to pass. When the birth takes place, it is at that point and time that the vision has become reality. What used to be vision is now reality as the mother holds that baby in her arms. Millennium Churches will be churches of reality. They will touch people at the point of their need. They will reach down into the gutters and the cesspools of life to rescue the perishing and care for the dying. Their theme song will be "Jesus Saves! Jesus Saves!" Services in these churches will house a sermon delivery that will present a message of grace that will be applicable to the people from all walks of life. They will know that no matter where they have come from that what is important now is where they are going! They will have a message that will be relevant for today. They will sing a song that the angels do not know how to sing. It will be the song of the redeemed. Therefore, the redeemed of The Lord shall return and come with singing unto Zion, and everlasting joy shall be upon their heads.

A Mother's Influence

Finally, the importance of the influence of a mother is necessary in The Millennium Church. A mother has a sense of protection over her young. She has the instinct to guard them and protect them from every evil if possible. She watches her children with a sharp eye and knows the steps that they may take. Even as the Mother eagle teaches her young to fly, she never takes her eyes off them. She stirs up the nest in order to make them try to fly. However, she remains within reaching distance, and if they begin to fall, she immediately swoops down to rescue them from their fall.

Jochebed, the mother of Moses is a good example of a mother's influence and care. She was determined to save her son from the hand of Pharaoh in his infancy. There was an onslaught to destroy this man of God even in his infancy. Pharaoh issued a decree that all of the male babies should be killed. God strategically orchestrated a plan that would take care of Moses and his mother Jochebed until the time came for Moses' destiny to come into focus and be fulfilled.

Her determination allowed The Lord to give her a strategy to save her son from being taken out before his time. God gave her a plan to hide Moses along The Nile River. The Nile River was known for its reptiles. Snakes, alligators, and water creatures were within reach at any time to devour Moses. However, God was proving just how much He was taking care of Moses, just by sailing him down The Nile River with the reptiles. God protected him by orchestrating that his mother become his nursemaid and get paid for taking care of Him! Isn't that just like God?

The same type of instance was true in the infancy of Jesus. Herod issued a decree that all of the male children be killed, and God simply spoke to Mary and Joseph and redirected the destiny of Jesus for a season, allowing Him to take a different pathway just for a season, so that He could be spared to complete the tasks and the mission that He was sent to the earth to do. Satan knows that if he can destroy someone powerful in his infancy, he can destroy the progress of the church of The Living God.

The Millennium Church will possess a Maternal instinct that will influence and protect the children that she will *bring forth* in birth. These churches will have an impact on the lives of those whom they will produce. It was partly the influence of Mary, the mother of Jesus, which caused Him to flourish from the time that he was 12 years of age. As He submitted to them, He became great in wisdom and stature. Thank God for the maternal instinct in the last day Millennium Church!

CHAPTER 4

The Militant Movement Church

Matthew 11:12; "From the days of John the Baptist until now, the Kingdom of Heaven suffers violence and the violent taketh it by force."(Leadership Bible, NIV).

There is no doubt that we are living just before the coming of Jesus Christ, and the Church is in the midst of warfare. There is consistent war in the Heavenlies and the Christian has an awesome responsibility to engage in the battle. God has put some powerful weapons within our hands, and He is teaching us to use them as never before. He has given us spiritual authority over defiance in the church today. The enemy is launching assignment after assignment against her. Still, she is standing strong and powerful. This is the fruit of the lips and heart of Jesus as He said to Peter, "Upon this rock, I will build my church and the Gates of Hell shall not prevail against it." The church is not and will not be defeated.

The church was God's idea. As Jesus walked upon this earth with His disciples in a time of training them, He was making preparation to put the church in their hands. Little did they know that He in essence was training them for war. He cut no slack with them as He poured The Word of God into them on a daily basis. He intrigued them with His parables, and they were totally astounded by His wisdom; yet He let them know in no uncertain terms that He was raising them as *disciples*, and they would soon become *apostles*.

Once they became apostles, they would exhibit a spiritual stamina, which they had never experienced. There would be new levels of spiritual demand upon them that would bring forth validation to their new levels of anointing. The anointing is not just passed around in a silver cup! The anointing is costly! There is a price to pay! The greater your anointing, the greater the demands of The Holy Spirit upon your life.

The Millennium Church of this militant caliber will literally drip with the 'Costly Oil'! They will be so greased up with this oil that they will be able to slip right through some of the tough places before they even have the time to realize what they have just walked through. They will have a fragrance about them that is like none that the world has ever experienced. They will not be ashamed of the fact that they are following Jesus and flowing in the anointing of The Holy Spirit. They will not allow themselves to be intimidated by flesh and will have a complete understanding of to WHOM they belong! This Millennium Church will be fully dependent upon the Holy Spirit to lead, guide, speak, and accomplish all that has been ordained for them to do by the Father!

Preparation For The Battle

The disciples walked into The Upper Room on the day of Pentecost as a *small embryo*. They walked out of The Upper Room as a *mighty army*. They entered the arena of The Holy Ghost as *mannerly ministers*.

They exited into the fields of harvest with a *militant mentality*! Jesus chose them as *disciples*. They were inaugurated by The Holy Ghost as *apostles*! Jesus was equipping their hands for war and their fingers to fight.

After they were filled with The Holy Spirit, the disciples permeated the streets of Jerusalem with the Gospel. Churches were being born everywhere on a daily basis. They were initiated by the power of The Holy Spirit from on high and introduced to the public in bold and rare fashion! These churches being raised up by the first apostles were not all fun and games. They suffered much persecution in the process. They were beaten, thrown in jail, falsely accused, stoned, and chased out of cities. Yet in their hearts they knew that according to Isaiah 54:17, "No weapon formed against me shall prosper, and every tongue that shall rise against me in judgment thou shall condemn, for this is the heritage of the servant of the Lord." (Leadership Bible, NIV).

They knew that the power on the inside of them was much greater than the opposition that they were experiencing from the outside at this point! Therefore, they had no fear, just a bold faith in God! These were people that would purpose in their hearts that even if it cost them their lives they will go forth in His Name, both conquering and to conquer!

Holy Spirit Tenacity

I Corinthians 1:28 "Shrink not from your call: though you consider yourself but a foolish and small thing; for I have chosen you to nullify the things that are."(Leadership Bible, NIV).

47

They were empowered to nullify traditions of men and bring forth a new platform for The Body of Christ. They were not just accepting militancy; they were accepting martyrdom. Some of the literally gave their physical life in order to birth the church. The apostles were the real 'birthing fathers'. They could not afford to have fear at any level now. They purposed in their hearts that they would not shrink back. They were in for the long haul. This same attitude of heart will flow from The Millennium Church. Jesus said to the apostles in Luke 10:18 & 19 "I was watching Satan fall like lightning from the sky. Behold, I have given you authority to tread upon serpents and upon scorpions, and over all the power of the enemy, and nothing shall injure you!" (Leadership Bible, NIV).

Then in verse 21, right after Jesus shared these things with His disciples, He prayed this prayer to the Father: "Father, Lord of Heaven and earth, I thank you because you concealed these things from the sophisticated and the educated, yet you revealed them to ordinary people. Yes Father, I thank you that it pleased you to do this!" (Complete Jewish Bible). The Millennium Church will be made up of congregations of people that will be very much aware of their inadequacies and yet depend fully upon The Lord for their abilities! They will just be ordinary people that God will use to bring about and to establish His ultimate plan, and to accomplish extraordinary things!

These people will not be those who have necessarily graduated from 'seminary' but they will have completed and graduated a prayer closet course with a Word from God. They will not care about what other people might think, as long as they are aware that they are walking in the approval of God. They are righteous, and they will not shrink back! They will pray and intercede until they accomplish break-through, and then they will look at the wondrous things that the Lord has done and rejoice in the presence of their enemies!

Wardrobe for Warfare

Ephesians 6:13 in the Complete Jewish Bible Translation, the Apostle Paul instructs us in this manner: "So take up every piece of war equipment that the Lord provides; so that when the evil day comes, you will be able to resist; then when the battle is won, you will still be standing! Therefore, STAND!"(Leadership Bible, NIV). In my spirit, I am convinced that The Millennium Church will use every piece of equipment that the Lord has ordained for us in this hour. There is such a price to pay for The Kingdom of God to receive ministry. We are living in a great day, but we are also living in the midst of a Spiritual War Zone. Whenever we stand nose to nose with the Devil and his demons and declare "Satan, this is war!" we cannot afford to be caught without our OWN equipment! Do not ever tantalize the devil unless you know what to do to take care of him!

Such was the case as David headed out to face Goliath. When he realized that Saul's armor did not fit him, he paused long enough to remove it so that it would not be a hindrance to him. He had not proven Saul's armor, so he knew that he could not use it. The church of this hour will have their own armor, tried and proven, by the fact they have won battle after battle. These are people that have an assurance in God and a confidence in His almighty power to take care of them in the midst of their battle. They will have had experiences throughout their lifetime that has proven to them time and time again the Lord is with them and never forsakes His own.

No one ever goes to war alone. Even the foxholes are made for double occupancy. The same is true in the things of The Holy Spirit. We are a team! Teams are more protected in the time of warfare. Before a wolf attacks a sheepfold, he takes a survey of the flock. If the pasture is full of sheep, he does not dare try to attack. However, if there is only one, he feels as if he can handle it and proceeds to go after the one sheep.

Likewise, David could not use Saul's armor, but by his experience, he had his own. David had Five Smooth Stones! As David had trusted in God before, he still trusted in God to let him pull the right stone out of his pocket to take Goliath down! He knew what it was to slay the lion and the bear with his own hands.

Paul exhorts us regarding our warfare wardrobe. Some people have the concept that if they need it they will carry it! Paul said, 'Have the BELT of TRUTH buckled around your waist!' The word truth means "actuality, authenticity, and accuracy." "Correctness, exactness, and honesty" are also some of the meaning of the word truth. If we look closely at David, he wore all of these! He definitely had accuracy, actuality, exactness and correctness when he finished with Goliath. David did not have to tell anybody how accurate he was in his warfare. Everybody saw, and everybody knew he was equipped with the right armor! This church will wear the right wardrobe, and carry the proper equipment for the battle before them.

The word buckled means to "fasten, collapse, and yield." Those three words within themselves could give us some powerful instruction. First of all, in the time of Warfare, there must be sure place, or a solid foundation. There can be no uncertainties in the time of spiritual warfare. The church has suffered many a casualty because we have gone into warfare unprepared for the battle. We must be sure that our spiritual feet are in an even place. Once we make that commitment, we cannot afford to look back.

The Millennium Church will be filled with intercessors that will have an ear to hear what The Spirit of The Lord is saying and will perform the actions of war that will protect The Body of Christ and have its best interests at heart. These intercessors will be prophetic intercessors, uninterested in making a name for themselves, but purposing to know that the will of The Lord is being accomplished.

They will have a unique ability to remain humble in the sight and the presence of The Lord and give way or 'collapse' to the will of God. These will not pray for their will, but for The Father's will to be done in the church. The Millennium Intercessor will have the heart of God and pray into existence the last day movement of The Holy Spirit; therefore, pushing out by the power of prayer and intercession, those things that are unlike God! They will be more than willing to 'Yield' to what the Father desires and be perfectly content in knowing that they are simply following His orders. What a powerful corporate army for The Body of Christ! They will definitely have the "truth buckled" around their waist and totally collapse to the desires of The Lord and yield themselves completely to The Father!

"Righteousness will be their breastplate and they will wear upon their feet the readiness that comes from knowing The Good News of Shalom. They will have the shield of trust at all times with which they can extinguish all of the Flaming Arrows of the Evil One! They will have at all times the Helmet of Deliverance, along with the Sword that is given by The Holy Spirit, that is the Word of God; as they pray at all times, with all kinds of prayers and requests, in the Spirit, vigilantly, and persistently, for all of God's people!" (Complete Jewish Bible).

This is definitely a unique wardrobe for warfare! The breastplate will cover the heart, becoming a bi-fold filtering system that will sift out impurities, protecting the heart from spiritual viruses that will try to invade and cause damage to the arteries of the church herself. At the same time, the breastplate of righteousness will produce a statement that we are covered with a mantle of purity that is unlike anything that the church has ever seen, even in her history!

Our feet will walk in peace knowing that our steps everyday are being ordered by The Lord and that everywhere He sends us He has already been. Any un-chartered waters that we have not yet sailed,

He is going before us; any enemy territory that has not yet been conquered, The Great Warrior Himself is going ahead of us with strategy and power to conquer the land and walk away from there with the plundering of the spoils! This Millennium Church will rest upon The Word of the Lord to Joshua when he said to him, "Every place that you put your FOOT, know that I The Lord will give it to you!"(Leadership Bible, NIV). We walk in peace with The Lord knowing that He is a shield about us!

Millennium Intercessors will have at their disposal the Shield of Faith, in order to snuff out all of the fiery darts, or the flaming swords, that the enemy will hurl at the church. They will not only possess the shield; they will be ultimately trained in how to use it! It must be moved from side to side, top to bottom, thrust forward at times and then drawn back for the proper usage. Whether the enemy is using subtle attacks or frontal assaults, The Millennium Church Intercessors and Warriors will know exactly what to do with the shield!

They will constantly wear the helmet of salvation or deliverance upon their heads. This will protect their minds and also keep the Enemy from sowing thoughts that are unlike The Lord; thoughts that come from Satan that remain in the soil of our minds become seed for a harvest of hurt, destruction, and heartaches for many people. They can be therapeutically plowed up. However, we can be preventative and never allow them to be planted by wearing the helmet of deliverance! The helmet of deliverance will cover the 'reins of our mind', that the Psalmist David tells us about, and protect us from such demonic activity. The Church of The Millennium will think on whatsoever things are true, lovely, honest, and of a good report! The helmet will close in around our spiritual ears and we will hear The Word of The Lord.

The helmet along with the sword of The Spirit, which is The Word of God, will be the lifeline of the Church in these last hours that we serve. For The Word of God is quick! We will need His Word to be applicable to us and our needs many times right on the spot! The Word of the Lord is powerful! We will be instant in season and out of season! We will not speak with enticing words of man's wisdom, but in the power and the demonstration of The Holy Ghost!

The Word of God is sharper than any two-edged sword! The Word of the Lord will be made readily available for us in the days ahead. That which we have stored up within our hearts and in the spirit man, will be brought back to our remembrance instantaneously. We must have The Word of God in our hearts and not just in our minds. It must be transferable! There has to be a sixteen-inch interchangeable bypass from the head to the heart at any given moment. It must come from the heart and not just from the lips! The head knowledge is a necessity, but there must be a working relationship between the heart, the head, and The Word of God in order to make The Word to work mightily within us.

Finally, The Millennium Church will be clothed with a mantle of prayer! They will pray without ceasing! They will pray always, with all prayer and supplication, lifting up holy hands, without wrath and doubting. They will pray in the spirit and the understanding also! They will be a people of prayer. The Millennium Church will be a people that will not make one decision without first making inquiry of the Lord, even as David did. They will pray all kinds of prayers such as intercession, supplication, petition, travail, mourning, lamenting, sackcloth and ashes, praise, adoration, thanksgiving, and repentance.

This people of prayer will perform actions that are sanctioned by prayer. The anointing will envelope all that they do because of the dependency upon The Lord and their willingness to hear from Him before they implement their own actions. They will pray forceful, vigilant prayers. They will keep a prayer upon their lips and The Word of God will be nigh within their heart and their accomplishments in The Kingdom of God will astound those who are watching. Jesus said to us in John, Chapter 15, "Apart from me, you can do nothing...." How true that statement!

We must as The Millennium Church, learn to be dependent upon the Lord and not our abilities alone. In our strength alone we will fail, but this last day church will have the mentality, "I can do all things through Christ who strengthens me!" (Leadership Bible, NIV).

This Millennium Church will be a militant movement upon the earth. She will march to the sound of the heart throb of God and never miss a step. Why? Because she is uniquely trained and equipped for the war ahead of her. Like The Bride of Christ in combat boots, she will walk into the midst of enemy territory and never shudder in fear, shrink back, or turn tail and run from the enemy. With her weapons intact and her soldiers trained and in position, she will have the game plan and the strategy that is necessary to set The Body of Jesus Christ free from the attacks of the adversary. She will be an intercessory church – a church that will be willing to take the bullet in order for The Kingdom of God to be formed within us.

We have sung a song for many years entitled "The Church Triumphant." However, we will never become the church triumphant until we become "The Church Militant."

The Millennium Church will arise for war!

Mighty Warrior Mentality

This Millennium Church people will have a warlike mentality. They will in no way accept anything that Satan may try to put upon them. They will have a hostile attitude toward the devil! Being able to stand their spiritual ground, they will appear to be very belligerent with the adversary. There comes a time that we need to get fed up with whatever the enemy may be trying to do to us or even work against us. This church will not tolerate the enemy crossing over upon their spiritual territory! They will draw a line in the sand. Jesus has already drawn a bloodline that no devil nor demon in hell has the power to cross over anyway!

People of this spiritual mentality will be antagonistic with Satan. It is an assignment from hell to keep the people of God so frustrated that they cannot complete the work that God has called and anointed them to do. We must never allow the enemy to break our focus! When Nehemiah was rebuilding the wall of Jerusalem, Sanballat and Tobiah sent for him to come and talk with them, as a ploy of the enemy just to break their focus and to frustrate their purpose!

We must, with the same resolve as Nehemiah, obey the command of Jesus by saying, "Get behind me, Satan!" (And don't you push!)

Nehemiah in his wisdom sent the word back to Sanballat and Tobiah, "I am doing a good work, and I cannot come down!" This will be the mentality of The Millennium Church. They will not give into the temptation of the devil, so they will learn how to just put him to silence at the onset of the battle! That does not mean that we will not have to fight once in a while. However, The Lord will give us the victory once we purpose in our hearts that the devil will not run over us, and neither will he override the ultimate plan of God!

These people of this type church will be opposed to giving the Devil any room! The Bible tells us to 'Give No Place To The Devil!' The people of God who will stand in opposition against their enemy will walk away from the confrontation as the victor and not the victim! The Millennium Church will be an aggressive fellowship that will be, and become, established in the things of God as never before! They will press into God without having to be told. They will know who they are in Christ Jesus and will not be intimidated by the tactics nor the schemes of the devil. They will realize that "in Him they are more than conquerors through Jesus Christ who loved us and gave Himself for us!" Their song will be Romans 8:31; "If God be for us, who can be against us?" (Spirit Filled Life Bible).

I am certainly not insinuating that the church will win every battle in the last days. However, what I am saying is that God will have a people who have already come through much tribulation and will be determined in their hearts to conquer their enemy as the "God of peace will bruise Satan under their feet shortly!" (Leadership Bible, NIV). This Millennium Church will be made up of kingdom personnel who will have a mighty warrior mentality! They will carry the titles of the five-fold ministry! They will be like David in Psalm 18 when he said, "I pursued my enemies and overtook them!"(Leadership Bible, NIV). That is what the Lord is waiting upon This Millennium Church to do! Come on Church! I hear a war cry coming forth! Pursue your enemy and defeat him. Engage him and finish the battle. Remember, "Greater is He who is in you than he who is in the world!" (Leadership Bible, NIV).

CHAPTER 5

The Mobile Church

Webster defines the word 'mobile' as meaning three different things: movable, portable, and free. Then there is scriptural collateral for this definition in John 8:36. "Therefore if the Son shall make you free, you shall be free indeed!"(Leadership Bible, NIV). Acts 17:28 says, "For it is in Him that we live, and move, and have our being....for we are His offspring!"(Leadership Bible, NIV). God does not live in bondage. He is not bound! He is FREE!! He is MOVABLE! He is PORTABLE! The Millennium Church will definitely be His offspring. They will be a people who will be free, pliable, and obedient in the hands of The Lord ready at the moving of the Glory cloud to pick up, to move, or to stay. Whatever The Lord required of them, that was what the children of Israel were willing to do. The Church of The Millennium will hear the voice of The Lord and be ready at all times to respond unto the Lord.

The word 'move' means to go, or to cause to go to another point. The Millennium Church will be progressive as well as aggressive in its pursuit of the will of God! Its people will be very dissatisfied if they are not allowed to move forward. Their zeal will require an outlet of some sort and the source of supply for the outlet needs to be the church fellowship of which they are a part. These people will feel the need to check the cloud every day. They will start packing when the cloud starts increasing or changing position.

In Numbers 9:15-23 we have the Biblical example of the cloud by day and the fire by night and its ability to MOVE whenever The Lord was saying such to the children of Israel. Verse 15 says, "Now on the day that the Tabernacle was raised up, the cloud covered the tabernacle, the tent of the Testimony; from evening until morning it was above the tabernacle like the appearance of fire…." (Leadership Bible, NIV). The Millennium congregation will not be satisfied with anything less than the fiery presence of The Lord in their church services. They will be a people who will be in hot pursuit of the presence of The Holy Spirit and no price will be too high to pay for the blessing! This people will be people of sacrifice and they will appreciate and respect the presence of The Lord in their midst. The words, 'comfort zone' will not be in their spiritual vocabulary. They will move consistently from faith to faith, strength to strength, and from glory to glory!

The intensity of the atmosphere of the worship services must change in order to experience the outpouring and the residence of The Holy Spirit in our midst. We must be willing to be mobile in The Spirit and to move with the cloud. When the cloud stays, we must stay. The agenda of our church services can be structured by man, but they must be ordered by The Holy Spirit. When the cloud moves in the worship services then we must learn to flow with the cloud. The children of Israel had to be willing to obey The Lord and Moses and move from time to time, from place to place. We could call this moving from faith to faith, strength to strength, and glory to glory!

One of the things that have paralyzed our churches in the past is the fact that we have never been willing to move when God said MOVE! The Millennium Church will change that mentality. This church will not be bound by the way we used to do things. They will be very spontaneous and liberal in the things of The Spirit and they will waste no time or cut no slack with the enemy!

The scriptures tell us in verse 16, "And so it was always; the cloud covered it by day, and the appearance of fire by night". (Verse -17); "Whenever the cloud was taken up from above the Tabernacle, after that the children of Israel would journey; and in the place where the cloud settled, there the children of Israel would pitch their tents." (Leadership Bible, NIV). They were never caught in a rut. They always were willing to Change! Every time they obeyed The Lord's command they were doing what is called an "advance". To advance means to bring forward or to promote. It means forward movement, improvement; being ahead of time.

They were indeed very portable. They had no other choice. God had continuously thrust them out of their passivity. They never knew how long they might be allowed to stay in any given place. They could be here today, and in another place tomorrow!

They were not filled with an abundant amount of AGGRESSIVE power only PROGRESSIVE power. There is a vast difference. However, there were times that even their progressive power had to be initiated by Moses himself. They were not very motivated at times. The Church of the 21st Century must be ready, willing, and able to be aggressive and progressive in their pursuits of The Lord. They will take action and step forth to achieve a goal or a dream! They will be achievers!

The word, "move" also means to change residence or position. I am reminded of Abraham in Genesis 12, as the Lord gives him instruction as to what he is supposed to do from that point in his life. God told Abraham to "Get out of his country, away from his family, leave your Father's house, and go to a land that I will show you….!" (Leadership Bible, NIV).

What a sacrifice on the part of Abraham! I am sure he was comfortable. He probably was not in the mood to make changes! Nevertheless, he was willing to hear The Lord and to move into the *destiny* that God had in store for him. Not only was he willing to move forward, he was also willing to let go! Many folks desire to move ahead, but they are just not willing to turn their backs on what used to be. We cannot press toward the north, if we are always looking toward the south! Many would have refused had God given us such a mandate for our ministry. The church of this day cannot afford to be satisfied with the status-quo! That mentality will change for The Millennium Church, and she will accomplish God's complete plan for her upon the earth!

Abraham was movable. He was portable. He heard the voice of The Lord and obeyed Him as he spoke. The 21st Century church must also be the same in order to be on the cutting edge of what The Holy Spirit is doing all throughout the land today. Daniel and the three Hebrew children were portable and movable. I am sure when they were deported they were unable to see God, or good, in their circumstances. However, it became the avenue through which The Lord worked to bring their promotion! It took a Pharaoh to create 'Movement in the children of Israel'. They had to become dissatisfied with their wilderness in order to move into their promised land!

Joseph was probably taken by surprise when his jealous brothers became furious with him regarding his dream. They threw him in a pit, took his coat of many colors, and sold him to an Ishmaelite Tribe for $12.80 in just a matter of hours. The ordeal appeared to be a tragedy, yet it was a pathway for Joseph in becoming promoted to The Prime Minister of Egypt one day!

Goliath was much bigger and more experienced than David, yet David knew he was the man for the job, so he moved forward. With one swing of a sling, David laid him to the ground, took his own sword and cut off his head, then took it back to camp with him to show it off! Victory looked impossible in the eyes of the onlooker, yet David was willing to change his position in order to fulfill God's will for his life! He was promoted afterward. It is called 'MOVING FORWARD IN ADVANCE!' or MOBILITY! Movable and Portable!

Then thirdly, is the word "free". One of the more visible attributes of The Millennium Church will be her level of freedom in the things of God. She will be free to worship God's way, free to grow without inhibitions of the philosophy of men; she will have an abundance for the sake of being free in her finances. Yet and still there must be a freedom to move on and go forward without falling and growing weary in the process over and over. Many churches have begun with good intentions, yet failed before reaching their goals. Why? They failed to prepare as well as neglected to take advantage of the resources that God has put before them as His people.

CHAPTER 6

The Mighty Warrior Church

The Horses and Horseman

The Bible declares to us that he whom the Son sets free is free indeed! During my travels the last several years, I have heard many professors, teachers, and lecturers compare the freedom of the church, as well as The Apostolic Movement of today, with the spirit of horses. In light of that, I began to do a little study on the activity of horses in the Bible. Much to my surprise, here is what I found!

There are several elements that are linked together in the stories of horses that I could research in The Word of God. Jeremiah 12:5 reads "If you have raced with men on foot, and they have wearied thee, how shall you compete with *horses?*" (Leadership Bible, NIV). I am about to give you a synopsis of what I believe to be one other link to the church of the 21st Century.

In Revelation 6:2-9; 8:1-5, there is a repetitive mention of horses. Horses are mentioned very often in The Bible, but were of very little importance to the average Hebrew. Hebrews found it more practical to keep a donkey to ride, or an ox to pull a plow. It seems to me that this is still the mentality of the church world today. Just get a donkey or an ox! That is all that we need! Yet the individuals who make up the church have grown weary in well doing just keeping up with the donkeys and the oxen. If we have grown weary running at a slow pace, how are we going to run with the horses? Their excuse sounds much like this: "We do not want to get ahead of God! We need to take this slowly! We just need to slow down for a while!" How many times have I heard that said throughout the course of my ministry!

God warned the children of Israel many times not to put their faith in the strength and the speed of horses (Psalm 20:7, Leadership Bible, NIV) or to even multiply their horses (Deut.17, Leadership Bible, NIV). Yet for whatever reason, David and Solomon built up a large mounted force by importing horses from other countries. Solomon had a large cavalry, as well as horses to draw war chariots. Then wherever there were horses, there had to be horsemen. Horsemen were sometimes used as mail carriers, (Esther 8:10, Leadership Bible, NIV), but for the most part, horses were thought of in terms of war. There will be an increase in the intensity of warfare as we enter the arena of the last days, just before the coming of Jesus. No kind of ministry will draw demonic forces like that of the apostle and the prophet. It just comes packaged with this anointing!

The Apostolic Movement that we are seeing today has great reference to the existence of horses. Horses are of a *free spirit*, and I am convinced they are relevant to the church today! One of the applications of the 'movable church', which I mentioned earlier on, was the ability to *'move ahead of time'*. This is the spiritual characteristic of the *office of the apostle*. Apostles are considered to be first in order, first in place and first in time. They are forerunners, path clearers, and way-makers. Apostles are visionaries and they sometimes see the full picture ahead. They not only see it, but they are graced with an ability to achieve it. They can lay out the spiritual architecture that is required to bring the vision to pass.

There were several other elements that I came across in my study of the horses. Of course, wherever there were horses, there had to be horsemen. We have already established that the horsemen were much of the time used as letter carriers. How we need Word of God carriers in the world today. Those who will take the letter of The Lord to places that are not easy to invade! Wow! What a Prophetic Word from God! Then along with the horseman, I came across seven other elements that I felt were important to This Millennium Church!

The Charioteer

A Charioteer was a soldier who fought from a chariot. Chariots were first introduced in Mesopotamia about 2000 B.C. They came in many different sizes and many different forms. Much like the churches of today! These machines served as *MOBILE FIRING PLATFORMS!* They could be two wheeled or four wheeled and drawn by either two horses or four horses. There will be a yoking of the five fold ministries in The Millennium. I believe that the two horses represent the Apostle and the Prophet being yoked together. The four horses are what I believe to the operation of all five-fold offices, or what some would describe as the four fold offices with Pastor/Teacher being termed as the same office.

Not only is God raising up apostles and prophets, evangelists and pastor/teachers as individuals, He is also raising up apostolic, prophetic, evangelistic, and pastor/teacher churches in order to minister to the 'whole person' in today's society. These types of churches are what I refer to as 'specialty churches'. Then there will be those who operate in all of the ascension gifts. As these mobile platforms in Bible days became more and more of use, they were being recognized as indispensable warfare vehicles and as technology developed, the chariots became more developed.

They started out small, but as time went on they increased in size. As they increased in size, they were enabled by The Holy Spirit to encounter more levels of warfare and at the same time, operate with protective covering. The Chariots themselves were eventually made to hold a driver, a bowman, and a shield bearer to protect the warrior and the driver! As they expanded, they equipped themselves to take care of their territory! They made sure that the charioteer, who I believe represents the pastors of our churches, were totally covered and protected from the fires of the war!

The mobility of the chariot enabled them to move about from place to place and to wage war on their enemy and with all necessary war equipment. The chariot, the horses, the horsemen, the charioteer, the bowman, and the shield bearer were willing to be *MOBILE*, and move from place to place, yet remain 'mighty' enough through their skills to win the war! In Solomon's day, he employed the most charioteers outside of Egypt. At one point, he deployed 1,400 chariots throughout the land in fortified 'Chariot Cities' (I Kings 10:26, Leadership Bible, NIV), and then later built 4,000 stalls for his horses and his chariots (II Chronicles 9:25, Leadership Bible, NIV)! How interesting! Would it not be a glorious thing to be able to release 1400 chariots into 1400 different cities throughout America and around the world, engaged in mighty warfare that would clean up the city, and prepare them for the planting of 4000 Millennium Churches before Christ returns? Praise God! What a vision!

The Soldiers

Even though Israel conquered the Promised Land by waging war, it did not have a standing army until the time of Solomon (I Kings 10:26, Leadership Bible, NIV). However, all 20-year-old males were on standby and were liable for emergency military duty. (Number 1:3, Leadership Bible, NIV). They were just a few exceptions to the rule. (Duet. 20:5-8, Leadership Bible, NIV), Saul maintained a body of chosen, capable fighters, (I Samuel 13:15, Leadership Bible, NIV), and David recruited a force of "Mighty Men" (I Samuel 22:2, Leadership Bible, NIV). Under the leadership of King David, each tribe had a well-delineated chain of command and trained its adult males to use military weapons. (I Chronicles 12, Leadership Bible, NIV). The Bible mentions several specific kinds of soldiers. Let's take a look at them as well as their job description.

The Guard

(Translated "Watchman")

The duty of a Watchman was to stand guard over or to watch over something of value, perhaps a treasure, a person, or a city. From the height and protection of a watchtower, a guard watched over cities and fields looking for thieves and ravaging animals. (Psalms 80:13; Song of Sol. 2:15, Leadership Bible, NIV). Nehemiah appointed watchman to guard the walls of Jerusalem during their rebuilding (Nehemiah 4:9, 7:3, Leadership Bible, NIV). Some watchmen also worked as guardians or policemen, patrolling the city. (Psalms 127:1; Song of Solomon 5:7, Leadership Bible, NIV). The Jews divided the night into three military watches, which the watchman was required to call out. (II Samuel 18:24-27; Isaiah 21: 11 & 12; Matt. 14:25, Leadership Bible, NIV). Under the Romans, they adopted the Roman method of dividing the night into four watches (Mark 13:35, Leadership Bible, NIV). In a Spiritual sense, prophets and teachers were appointed watchmen to keep His people morally alert. (Ezekiel 33:2-7; II Timothy 4:5, Leadership Bible, NIV).

The Millennium Church will be that which will house, train and release prayer warriors who will guard the treasures within The House of God, people, and their cities. They will be alerted whenever there is danger on the way. Much to the dissatisfaction of the pastor, Millennium Intercessors will not stay locked into the church as in the past. They will feel the need to be released to go and pray, maybe days and weeks at the time. They will also need the freedom to go to other churches and pray for them, not just their own fellowship.

They will have wisdom to know when the devil wants us to stop building the wall and will advise in that; they will know how to spiritually patrol their cities and call out the dangers. They will not mind keeping the military watches or even the around the clock 24 hour watches that will be necessary, such as at the tomb of Jesus! Finally, there will be prophets and teachers that will guard the people of God to have and maintain a pure heart!

The Body Guards

Many of the 'body guards' mentioned in the scriptures were also known as soldiers, slaves, prison guards, runners, or servants. After Joseph's brothers sold him into slavery, Potiphar, who was a captain of the guard, and an Egyptian purchased Joseph. Then when Potiphar's wife wrongfully accused Joseph of sexually violating her and he was thrown into prison, Pharaoh threw the chief butler and the chief baker into the house of the 'Captain of the Guard', where Joseph was already confined.

The Bodyguards in this instance were actually drawn to Joseph by The Lord, and he was given great favor in their sight. The Millennium Church must be made up of people who know who they are in God and walk in the favor and the integrity of The Lord! These folks who will fill our church fellowships in these days, will be scarred, broken, mutilated by their pasts, and yet because of the favor of God and protection over their lives, their church fellowship may be their avenue for God to allow them to reach their Destiny! In Joseph's situation, he should have been executed. Yet his imprisonment was evidence that Potiphar apparently did not fully believe his wife in her accusation against Joseph.

As this body of believers, we must make up our minds and purpose in our hearts that we are going to be required of God to be each other's 'bodyguards'. We must operate in integrity, obtain the favor of God and man, and as much as lies within us, live at peace with all men! God can bring people around us and give us such favor with them; they will protect us from anything that the enemy may try to orchestrate against us. Thank God for The Millennium Church bodyguards.

II Samuel 23:20-23 tells us "Benaiah was the son of Jehoiada, the son of a valiant man from Kabzeel, who had done many deeds. He had killed two lion – like heroes of Moab. He also had gone down and killed a lion in the midst of a pit on a snowy day. And he killed an Egyptian, a spectacular man in appearance. The Egyptian had a spear in his hand; so he went down to him with a staff, wrestled the spear out of the Egyptian's hand, and killed him with his own spear. These things Benaiah the son of Jehoiada did, and won a name among three MIGHTY MEN! He was more honored than the thirty, but he did not attain to the first three. And David appointed him over his guard." (Spirit Filled Life Bible)

In this chapter of II Samuel, there is a list of the elite warriors of David's personal bodyguard and special royal forces. The Scripture gives forth clarity and definition to the talents of this soldier, Benaiah. However, even in all of his accomplishments, there were still areas of service for which he was not yet prepared. David had the spiritual wisdom to discern this. As we reach out to protect one another, the leadership of The Millennium Churches must be extremely wise and discerning as to where to position people within

The Body of Christ. Otherwise, we will be putting them in extreme danger as well as the church.

As gifted as Benaiah was, his opportunities had not yet yielded him the experience that was needed to be a captain. Yet David saw his gift and talent as being more than sufficient to take care of his guard, so he appointed him to the position. He was a mighty man, but he had to stay within his boundaries and perform there until he became more seasoned. The church in the last hours of her time upon the earth will need all levels of guarding by The Holy Spirit. We must remember that The Holy Spirit works through you and me. Pastors must use extreme caution in the choosing of leadership now more than ever. Everyone who says that they want to help us build is not always sent to us by God. Satan, our adversary, sometimes will try to plant those among us who have come with a plan to do nothing less than 'frustrate our purpose' (Ezra 4:4&5, Leadership Bible, NIV). They will only be looking for a place to pacify and fulfill their lust for manipulation, control, and power. This type of people, unless kept under a strong hand of leadership, will have the ability to 'bewitch' the people of our congregations, (Galatians 3:1-5, Leadership Bible, NIV), gain their approval, and then create a schism within the body when they are not allowed to have their way.

These people of this caliber will have symptoms of legalism, not grace. They will have a desire to operate by the law alone without The Holy Spirit at work as well. I am not saying that this personality of church cannot be used in The Millennium. I believe that they can and will be used. However, their effects upon their community or even those within the walls of the church will not be that of positive results.

Should this type thing take place? The spiritual alarm system of our inner man should warn us that there is danger up ahead. An application of leadership wisdom will initially not allow such people to occupy position, and therefore, will automatically release the leadership from having to dismiss them from certain roles they should never have held in the first place. Pastors and leaders have no choice at this point other than to protect their sheep at whatever cost. That is why we must have mighty men and women, and there must be spiritual bodyguards all around us.

The Archers

Archers were trained in and from their childhood. The Millennium Church will put great emphasis upon the children of their congregations. God is in the process of raising up an untarnished generation through our youth and children. In the beginning years of my public ministry, working with children was one of the first areas that God placed me in. I did Kid's Crusades year round for various events, and I would see these children making progress with The Lord. Some of them today are in ministries of some sort, which is very gratifying to me. However, more importantly than my gratification, they are fulfilling their call and destiny by God!

We must begin to train them in and from their childhood for the sake of the call of God that may be upon their lives. Just like the archers, they may have a mandate from God that will require special gifts and abilities that must be nurtured and channeled in the proper vein for them to become achievers. Once these archers were trained in the Old Testament, they became MIGHTY WARRIORS and were the first to ENGAGE the enemy from a distance. They were able to see him coming!

The Millennium Church will raise a Josiah Generation, and a Samuel Generation that will have ears to HEAR and eyes to SEE what the enemy is up to and then outwit him to cancel his assignment against the people of God! Several months ago, I heard The Lord say very plainly to me, "I am raising up a people who know how to conquer as well as do warfare. I have many people who are stranded in the second heaven who are always warring, but never conquering. When I raised up Joshua, I put within him a war cry that released an authority to conquer. I am about to do it again!" As I heard The Lord speak that to me, I rejoiced in my heart for how we need that ability to do warfare and then walk away with the spoils of it! God grant that to the church is my prayer!

Drawing an ancient war bow required the strength of at least a 100-pound pull. My interpretation of that would say that our youth are going to need a strength and an anointing from The Lord such as they have not seen activated upon this earth. There is going to be a supernatural anointing to reach and restore older generations as well as bring in the new generations. When an arrow was shot at that speed, it could pierce almost any armor. I believe that The Millennium Church will be a glorious church. At the same time I believe that we will experience some things in warfare that will utterly astound us. The Kingdom of Heaven suffers violence and the violent taketh it by force. We must raise up some archers from their youth in order to attack and pierce through the darkness any armour, both familiar and unfamiliar.

The Armor-bearer

Next, let's talk about the armor-bearer. The armor-bearer carried military weapons for a military commander or champion. They were responsible for finishing the job of killing enemies brought down by their masters, using either clubs or swords. There were many Old Testament leaders who had their own armor-bearers such as Abimelech in Judges 9:54. His armor-bearer was quick to obey his command as he instructed him to take his life from him. In I Samuel 14:6-17, Jonathan had his armor-bearer right by his side, even in all of his decisions. Verse seven says, "So his armor-bearer said to him, Do all that is in your heart. Go then. Here I am with you, according to your heart." (Leadership Bible,NIV). An armor-bearer was more than just an aide or servant, but he was a loyal partner in battle. They were very protective.

The Millennium Church Leadership will need such armor-bearers of such a caliber that they are willing to lay down their lives if necessary for those whom they serve. Protection is a must in all areas of both leaders, and laity. Physical, spiritual, material, financial, emotional areas are places that must be guarded well! No holes in the armor can be allowed by those whom we trust to serve us in this capacity especially in this hour that we live!

In II Samuel 18 (Leadership Bible, NIV), we read the story of the defeat and death of Absalom, David's son. Absalom had committed treason against his own father. He was politically positioning himself to undermine his father David's kingship, by stealing the hearts of men and women in the gates of the city. He declared how qualified he was, making his own father look bad in the eyes of the people who really mattered. He made sure that he was in the eyes of the people consistently and was making perpetual political strides against his own father.

In II Samuel 18:9-15 (Leadership Bible, NIV), we see how The Lord took matters into His own hands. God has no intention in these last days of letting "spiritual politicians" hold office in HIS Church! Absalom rode his mule underneath a terebrinth tree and his hair caught in a thick bough. His mule kept on riding, leaving him hanging in the tree by the hair of his head!

He was still alive, but Joab thrust three spears into his heart. In verse 18, the ten young men who bore Joab's armor, or his *armor-bearers*, surrounded Absalom and struck and killed him. The armor-bearers of today must have a keen eye and learn how to outwit the scheme of the enemy over those whom they serve.

In I Samuel 16:21(Leadership Bible, NIV), David acted as Saul's armor-bearer for a time. However, after David became King, commanders fought from chariots and armor-bearers were less needed. Armor-bearing is a ministry that is once again being implemented into the lives of our leaders by divine mandate of The Holy Spirit! Every church and leader needs this type ministry in operation.

The Armorer

This person was a blacksmith who was skilled in making armor or a leather worker who made shields. In the days of Saul, Hebrew soldiers made use of shields, helmets, breastplates of scale like plates and leg armor. The Apostle Paul speaks of the whole armor of God that must be worn by the spiritual soldier. I believe in The Millennium Church of this hour, that the armorer has relevance to the prophetic intercessor. In prophetic intercession, the intercessor sees what The Lord is doing. They have the full perspective of the plan of God and, therefore, they pray it into existence.

Whenever armor is worn, it must be an exact fit. Without a proper fitting, there will be places upon the body that will not be covered and, therefore, go unprotected. The reason David could not wear the armor of Saul was because it did not fit him. To be fitted for something, there has to be extreme detail and precise application. The prophetic intercessor will pray forth and into existence the extreme detail needed for the success of The Millennium Church and will know the precise application of the different types of prayer that will be needed. This way, the armor will be an exact fit for those who are filling this post of duty!

The Captain

The term captain in the Bible can mean more than one thing. It can have reference to a prince, officer, chief, ruler, leader, author, initiator, or commander. In The New Testament period, military captains commanded as many as 1000 Roman soldiers constituting a military cohort, tribune, or garrison. A garrison was a fort, or a company of soldiers that were stationed as a fort. They were actually a protective force over their own. They were stationed with a specific job description.

There was no question about what their particular duty was. They were to be on guard and remain ready at all times for rescue or defense in behalf of those they were assigned to protect. In The Millennium Church, there will be those who have the assignment to protect those who are in leadership.

They may be on sight or they may have the assignment to pray remotely. Whichever the case, they must remain alert in The Spirit and be very attentive to what The Lord is saying at any given point and time. In II Corinthians 11:32 (Leadership Bible, NIV), The Apostle Paul was rescued from an angry mob by a garrison of soldiers. These must have eyes to see, and ears to hear what The Spirit of The Lord is saying to the church.

This number of soldiers could vary between 600 to 6000. The Millennium Churches will be categorized as large, medium, and small. The larger the church is, the larger the garrison must be. The level of warfare will be much greater in large churches than in the medium or smaller sized church. The more sheep that you have, the more mess there is to clean up!

Then there were civilian captains in government who were called magistrates. They had a responsibility to bring peace to the cities, and to keep order. "Blessed are the Peacemakers, for they shall see God!" (Leadership Bible, NIV). They knew how to administer discipline to those who needed it and remain in good standing with others during the process. The Millennium Church needs the kind of wisdom that will enable us to make wise decisions when necessary. Wisdom is the principal thing, according to Proverbs!

We must have people within These Millennium Churches who will guard the cities where our churches are stationed! If we are ever going to grow our churches, then we must first see the need to take the city for God! The church is more than a building. The church is the people! We must have watchmen upon the walls of our churches sounding out an alarm in the times of danger and proclaiming triumph in the time of victory. Those to whom we can say "Watchman, what of the night? Watchman, what of the night?"

The Centurion

Then finally, there was the Centurions. The Centurion was the backbone of the relatively small, but well-organized citizen army of Rome. (Mark 15:39, Leadership Bible, NIV). A centurion was a non-commissioned officer who was the leader of at least one hundred men. All of the centurions in The New Testament were reported to have been men of good repute, and even exceptional faith.

In Luke chapter 7 (Leadership Bible, NIV), Jesus commended a Centurion who oversaw and cared for his dying servant. The Millennium Church must be filled with Centurions that will care for those who are hurting, and reach out in exhortation and encouragement.

The centurion who oversaw the crucifixion confessed faith in Jesus. (Matthew 27:54, Leadership Bible, NIV). In the book of Acts, the centurion Cornelius embraced the Gospel and opened the door to the Gentiles in the early church (Acts 10, Leadership Bible, NIV). The Millennium Centurions must be affected by the Gospel in order to affect others with the Gospel.

Just as Cornelius, they must be willing to go, do and speak The Word of God to all people who will listen, and even those who refuse. We have to be available to open doors of opportunity and then walk through those doors. Lastly, a Centurion named Julius saved the life of the Apostle Paul. The Millennium Church will be filled with those in position who are not just seeking for a title, but those who take their responsibility seriously and are willing to lay their lives down for the Gospel's sake and for others if deemed necessary.

To be a part of The New Millennium Church will be a wonderful opportunity, but there will also be sacrifice on the parts of those who will make up these unusual bodies. The Spirit of Joshua and Caleb must rest upon This Militant Church in this hour.

CHAPTER 7

The Musical Church

The Millennium Church will be filled with the sound of music. Music plays such an important role in the life and functions of our church bodies. Many churches suffer in this particular area, simply because there are so many different styles and we have the tendency to become locked into a certain way of doing things, including music. In Ephesians 5: 18 & 19, the Apostle Paul encourages us to "Be not drunk with wine wherein is excess, but be filled with the spirit, speaking to one another in psalms, hymns and spiritual songs, singing and making melody in our heart to the Lord." (Leadership Bible, NIV). The Millennium Church will have a core of people within it that will love to praise The Lord and will know by experience the power of the 'song'.

The more traditional churches may prefer the hymns, whereas the contemporary churches may prefer the psalms and spiritual songs. Whichever the case may be, inevitably the anointing must take over and favor the song and the music if we expect it to affect peoples' lives! I am convinced that we have never thoroughly understood the clarity and the definition of these three types of music. Let me expound upon these for just a moment.

The Psalms

The 'Psalms' are simply defined as *SCRIPTURAL LYRICS IN SONG*. The Psalms were used as the Jewish songbook. There is no more powerful a song that can be sung, than The Word of God. As we sing The Word, several things are happening. First of all, the spoken Word of God is *POWER!* The power of God is released into our services in a very unique way. The Millennium Church is a church that operates in the power of The Spirit of The Lord. Therefore, we must practice singing The Word of God in order to bring forth a release of His power in our midst.

Secondly, as we sing The Word of God, we are singing the WILL OF GOD! When we sing the will of God, it is the same as singing *'Thy Kingdom Come, Thy Will Be Done, On Earth As It Is In Heaven!'*(Leadership Bible, NIV). Whatever we are praying to happen upon the earth must first be born in the spirit realm. As we praise The Lord, our praise will release what is birthed in the spirit realm, and then we can call it to earth through our praises to The Lord!

Thirdly, as we sing The Word of God, we are allowing ourselves to *memorize Scripture.* One of the most effective ways to memorize The Word of God is by setting it to music! Sometimes we find it easier to remember a song rather than a text. The Millennium Church must be a people of The Word! Hebrews 4:12 says, *"For the Word of God is living and powerful, sharper than any two-edged sword, piercing even to the division of the soul and spirit, and of joints and marrow, and is a discerner of the thoughts and the intents of the heart."* (Spirit Filled Life Bible). As we walk, live, speak, sing, declare, The Word of God, it will reveal to us the very intentions of our soul where God is concerned.

We must be a people in the last days that will be a walking Bible. The day may come, should Jesus tarry, that our actual Bibles could be taken from us. Should that happen, we would only have what we have stored up from the Word into our hearts and minds by reading, studying, singing, preparing, and practicing. Man may be able to remove our Bibles from our hands, but he will never succeed in removing it from our hearts! Hallelujah!

The Hymns

Hymns are *'HUMANLY INSPIRED LYRICS IN SONG.'* Some of the greatest songwriters of our time have penned the most powerful of songs, such songs as *'Blessed Assurance'*, *'Great Is Thy Faithfulness'*, *'Tis So Sweet To Trust In Jesus'*, and *'When We All Get To Heaven'*. These have been the criteria for the blessing of many souls throughout the ages of time. There is no justifiable reasoning for ridding our churches of these type songs. The Millennium Church will be one that has a *'BALANCE'* in the way in which it operates. The writers of these songs, which I have mentioned, surely had relationship with God. I would think it is a tragedy to eliminate such profound insight in song from our church fellowships during the last days of the church upon the earth.

We would do no less than commit soul robbery for those around us who need to experience the touch of God through these touching lyrics of the old hymns. Many times such songs were written, not just through relationship with The Lord, but also through personal experience. Being a songwriter myself, I can tell you that nothing takes the place of those nights that God just wakes me up with inspiration and anointing. In just five short minutes, He can pen a song that is *SPIRITUALLY INSPIRED* that will change a life, cause a body to be healed, set a captive free, and allow us to *PRAISE* The Lord with our whole heart!

The Spiritual Songs

The *SPIRITUAL SONGS* that are mentioned here by The Apostle Paul are defined as *"Impromptu rhythmic lyrics given by The Holy Spirit in one's language or tongues."*

I Corinthians 14:15 says, "...I will sing with the spirit, and I will also sing with the understanding." (Leadership Bible, NIV). What was Paul talking about? He was simply revealing to us the place of tongues in his own personal prayer life. Praying in tongues is praying from the spirit, not our intellect. The exact same thing is true in regards to singing praises to The Lord. For Paul, praying and singing, both in tongues and in his very own language, were just normal and regular parts of prayer and praise. This has nothing to do with euphoria, hysteria, emotionalism, or abnormality of any kind. For this great spirit filled Apostle, it was simply a lifestyle of praise!

The Millennium Church will be open and active in singing such praises to The Lord. Yes, they will sing in tongues! Yes, they will even sing songs that flow from their hearts, and not a songbook! (Nothing is wrong with songbooks!) Yes, they will write them as they sing them for they will not just be another song. These types of spiritual songs will be birthed out of the joy and ecstasy of The Holy Spirit. *They will permeate our worship atmosphere with adoration and passion for the Father Himself as the people of God take the time to STARE into the face of Him whom their soul loves!*

These types of songs and music will be necessary to bring forth a new favor to the praise of Millennium Churches. *There will be prophetic songs, songs of travail, mourning, and lamenting; songs of joy and laughter; and songs of supplication and intercession!* This powerful gathering of people will release an aroma of spiritual incense to the Father that will move Him into the midst of His people in a fresh and unique way!

Highest Level of Faith

Praise is the highest level of faith in all of the earth. Why? It is because praise will give a person tunnel vision. Praise will refuse to see how bad or difficult a situation may be. It gives a clear unlimited focus on how God is working in the midst of circumstances. Praise has the potential to make a person's feet like hinds feet in high places! It will exercise spiritual muscles and give the spiritual energy to, as David said, 'Run through a troop and leap over a wall!' Singing a song unto The Lord will elevate the worshiper to spiritual plateaus that will cause him to soar like an eagle. Isaiah described it like this, "...They will mount up with wings as eagles, they shall run and not be weary, and they shall walk and not faint." (Leadership Bible, NIV). Singing praises unto The Father will keep a person moving in the spirit. Even when things in the natural look like they are not coming together, the power of musical praise will cause our spirit man to run, soar, leap and dance in the midst of it all. There really is power in the song of praise!

A Destructive Force

As we pursue our relationship with The Lord, there will be a time of experiencing battles so strong in our lives that we will not be able to PRAY. There have been many times in my life when I reached a certain point and said, "God, I do not know how to pray over this anymore. I have done, said, and prayed all I know to pray. So now, what am I to do?" The Lord has said to me many times, "I know you have prayed and I have heard. Just PRAISE me now for the answer!" When the enemy attacks us so strongly at times, and we do not know how to pray, or even feel like we cannot pray any more, he can cause us to move into a failing position. If we are in a failing position, we can lose the battle. That is what Satan wants to happen to you and me. So therefore, we must outwit Him!

How? Singing, playing our instruments, dancing before The Lord with all of our might….when we do these things, God will begin to flood our dark atmospheres with light. Praise will dispel darkness. Once our pathway is filled with light, even the light of the world, Jesus Christ; darkness has to go! The enemy is instantly exposed as soon as Jesus shows up. There is not enough room in your circumstance for both Jesus and the Devil. So when light comes forth, darkness loses its power and has to go! Musical praise will become a destructive force for you because it moves God into your situation. Prayer moves mountains, but praise will move God!

Praise Gives License to Angels

Praise will literally give license to angels. It releases heavenly forces into your situation to change the environment around you. It puts you into a position that will cause demonic forces to move away from you, or back away. Music and praise have a propelling force that will launch you from a defeated position into a place of victory. God has given us music and praise as a weapon that will cause our circumstances to yield to The Holy Spirit and what He has ordained for our life. The Millennium Church will be marching into the enemy's territory frequently for the purpose of defeating him and taking the spoils that belong both to it and to others who are babies in the Lord and are not yet strong enough to do battle for themselves. This is a pathway to victory. This church will be The Church Militant that will become The Church Triumphant.

Courts of Praise

Once we enter into His gates with thanksgiving we can enter into the courts of praise. Once we become thankful, we initiate praise. The Psalms tell us to 'Give thanks unto the Lord and bless His name!' Praise was never initiated to make us thankful. We must first become thankful and then, "Bless His Name!" There is so little thankfulness among people today. We have been so blessed that I think sometimes we take too much for granted. We should live a lifestyle of thanksgiving to The Lord with each new day! Thanksgiving opens the way for us to praise Him with a joyful heart. You must remember that The Holy Spirit is voice activated! That means that the more you shout, the more God stirs! The louder we praise Him, the larger He becomes in our midst. He is waiting on an intercessory praise voice – that voice just might be yours. You could hold the keys to a spiritual breakthrough for yourself, your church, or a worship service.

Bring Out the Band!

Psalms 148-150 (Leadership Bible, NIV), give to us explicit guidelines on how we are to praise the Lord in various areas of our lives. Psalm 150 (Leadership Bible, NIV), instructs us to 'Bring Out the Band!' We are to praise Him in the sanctuary, and the firmament; and to do it with the sound of the trumpet, the lute and the harp, timbrel and dance, stringed instruments and flutes. Praise Him with loud cymbals, even clashing symbols! Satan for so many years has tried to feed the church a lie. He has tried to make us believe that God does not like rhythm. I find that absurd. In the Book of Psalms, Asaph was the Chief Musician and he was a drummer! He was the head leader of all rhythm!

God likes rhythm! God created this world on a rhythmic system. He performed the construction of the earth one day at a time and set it up on clockwork. The stars sang a song while God created the world. God framed the heavens and the earth to the timing of a song. He wrote the song that the birds sing and then taught them how to sing it! Do you have any idea what a song does? A song is designed to take a person on a trip. They are written to take the listener, hook him for a while, as someone tells him the story in musical form. That is why it is so important that whatever kind of musical trip a person takes, the music takes him higher rather than lower.

It is important that we choose carefully to what we listen and meditate upon. Simply because we are infiltrated with what we expose our ears, minds, eyes, and hearts to including television, radio, and books. We must be careful that the sounds we allow to come into our ears be filled with The Spirit of God!

A Tri-Dimensional Force

Music is a tri-dimensional force that is built exactly like God Himself! It has melody, harmony, and rhythm, just like The Father, Son, and The Holy Ghost. It operates on the law of the square; one can put a thousand to flight; two can put ten thousand to flight. Heaven is continually filled with music and praises. Musical praise will also operate as a law of lift, lifting us up in our hearts and spirits. When we feel overwhelmed, the best thing that we can do is to sing unto The Lord a new song!

Anything that God touches makes a sound! Jesus told His disciples that if they refused to praise Him that the rocks would cry out. I refuse to let a rock take my place. If everything that God touches makes a sound, then whenever God touches me I need to shout! This will be The Mentality of The Millennium Church. At the touch of God, there will be a war cry of praise that will come forth from these churches!

The Millennium Church will have the high praises of God in their mouth continually. Pentecostal tradition says "I will not praise God until God moves me! I am waiting on God!" Well, God is waiting upon the church to arise with praise in their hearts and upon their lips in a sound of joyful praise and musical advancement! People who are indoctrinated with religion instead of salvation, will be those who will try to thwart the very purpose of God in the areas of the music in our churches! That is because they are numb to the sound of praise! Legalism will nullify the power of praise in our midst. We cannot afford that spirit to dwell or linger. As we exalt The Lord, those principalities will have to move from their place and succumb to The Holy Spirit!

Music in the Church

Music in the church is not for our entertainment. It is not for our enjoyment. It is for the sole purpose of bringing glory to God! Churches that are built upon entertainment have no strength. Strength only comes to the church as she magnifies and exalts the Name of The Lord. Where Jesus is exalted and lifted up, He said that He would draw all men unto Him! Just know that the sounds that come out of you are the sound of God. God did not create the Music. God is the music!

Music Announces Salvation

Luke 15:25 says, *"Now his older son was in the field. And as he came and drew near to the house, he heard music and dancing...." (Leadership Bible, NIV).*

Whenever a sinner is saved, the heavens ring with music and praises. The prodigal son had returned home to his father and they were in the midst of a celebration. Music always accompanies celebration. Even on birthdays and anniversaries, people will inevitably sing

'Happy Birthday or Anniversary.' Music has the potential to create an atmosphere of rejoicing and lightheartedness.

The people who were celebrating the return of the prodigal were singing, dancing and making music. Even though the elder brother had a joyless attitude, he still responded to the sound of the music and singing and was drawn to the celebration. The Millennium Church will be capable of having such atmospheres of celebration. Their music will not only celebrate those who find Christ as their Savior, but at the same time, it will have the potential to draw the people who have loveless, joyless, uncompassionate attitudes, and help them to make changes in their lives.

Music Drives Away Evil Spirits

I Samuel 16:23 says, *"And so it was, whenever the spirit from God was upon Saul, that David would take a harp and play it with his hand. Then Saul would become refreshed and well, and the distressing spirit would depart from him…"* (Leadership Bible, NIV).

This distressing spirit from The Lord tells us that when men and women depart from God, there is a vulnerability to evil spirits. God is sovereign in all realms, both physical and spiritual. However, if we fail to submit to Him, we are no longer protected from evil and its destruction. Saul is not just suffering from a depressed mental state with great anxiety; he is being *driven* by and evil spirit! David's music, because, '…The Lord is with Him', has the power to drive out the evil spirit. As David played his harp, he drove back the forces of darkness.

The same is true with The Music of The Millennium Church. There will be times that these churches will have demon possessed people in their midst and the music will be the heavenly brigade that will march forth and rescue the innocent as well as bring deliverance to the guilty! Also, music will be one of the keys that open the way for God to move into our midst and eliminate principalities and powers from the atmosphere.

At the very sound of music and praise, demons have to flee! Praise has been ordained that we might 'STILL THE ENEMY AND THE AVENGER'. That means that whenever we lift our voices or play our instruments, we are paralyzing the movements of Satan against us in all areas of our lives! We short-circuit the plans of the enemy as we sing, dance, and praise The Lord! Music is a tool to change the course of your battle. Praise is given to us for the sake of silencing our enemy!

The Holy Ghost is voice activated by the people of God. He is waiting upon an intercessory voice to move His Hand and also heart. Intercessory Praise is an important element needed in order for God to move in our midst. Praise is the trigger that causes the artillery of Heaven to be activated if you pull it! Neither demons nor darkness can survive in the sounds of praise! The Millennium Church will be filled with the tools and the artillery to take The Kingdom of Heaven by force on the keyboard, on the guitars, on the drums, and on the high sounding cymbals! Let everything that hath breath, "Praise Ye The Lord!"

CHAPTER 8

The Multiethnic Church

When I was a little girl growing up in the church, we never saw ethnic groups of people enter our doors. Why? It's simply because we have always had a tendency to put up walls against things or people that we do not understand or maybe disagree with. The Body of Christ has struggled with Prejudice Issues ever since its inception. Today, the acceptance of Ethnic groups has begun to change. Although there are still a few who do not have any desire for mixed congregations, the majority of churches understand that it is necessary if we are going to be in the divine will of The Father. It seems as though we are constantly having Conferences and Seminars in order to teach others how to grow Ethnic Churches. Ethnic situations are just not an issue with God. Jesus said, "And I, if I be lifted up from the earth, I will draw all men unto me." (Leadership Bible, NIV). One of the keys to solving ethnic issues is to understand that we are all one in Christ. There is one Lord, one faith, and one baptism, Father of all. Prejudice is not a "CHURCH" issue. Prejudice is a "Heart" issue. There are things that we must deal with within the heart before they will ever be settled within the church, and multiethnic issues are at the top of our lists.

The Blood of Jesus is compatible with all people because we are His offspring. His Royal Blood flows in us, and no matter what, the blood of Jesus is efficacious for everything. God is The Father of all, Jesus Christ is an International Savior, and The Holy Spirit is multilingual! He speaks in any language that He so desires!

All we have to do is take a long look at a map of our modern world. To do so, causes us to recognize the impact of racial and ethnic differences. The North, South, East, and West are laced with wars, conflicts, and problems that are tied to long-standing ethnic tensions. Living in a pluralistic society, we must understand that The Word of God has explicit and enormous implications for how we are to relate to people from other cultures.

When dealing with ethnic issues, we must remember that Jesus Himself had Global Connections. He preached a Global Gospel. In Jesus, we can all find hope, no matter what our background may be. We cannot touch 'Society', if we have prejudice in our hearts. For God so loved the world, that He gave His only begotten Son, that whosoever believeth in Him should not perish, but have everlasting life. In The Book of Acts we read where everyday people filled with God's love and power, apply their faith to life and society. This Book of the Bible had a Message that became a movement!

Old Testament Voices on Ethnicity

Moses

God's strategy in the beginning was to bring His blessing upon the entire world. He then singled out a one man and his family in order to accomplish His purpose. In Genesis 11:10 (Leadership Bible, NIV), God raises up a man named Abram later to become Abraham, through the bloodline of Shem. Just one man, but through him all of the NATIONS of the earth would be blessed. God has always intended blessing upon the entire world.

Moses married an Ethiopian woman and created conflict with family members and brought a crisis upon his nation. Numbers 12 implies that the root of this attack on Moses was racial intolerance. Moses siblings began to attack him because of his choice of wife. Ethiopia was filled with a dark skinned population of Africans that were sometimes entwined with the Egyptians. Moses could have met her during his years in Egypt, or she could have just been among the mixed multitude of people who journeyed with the Israelites out of Egypt. Aaron and Miriam actually used a Racial foundation to voice their opinion of their brother's place of leadership and authority. This rupture in leadership made God angry and He called the two of them on the carpet. He made it very clear to them that He was in charge and that He would communicate with whomever He chose to. His chosen was Moses. Aaron and Miriam were secondary.

Racism is an ugly sin and although God greatly disapproves, some of the very best of people struggle with this. Miriam instantly became a leper, and the entire nation of Israel had to bring its journey to a halt until she was restored. We must understand that when we touch the people of God we are playing with fire! Racism allows a point of entry for other ugly sins, which God will deal with, just as He dealt with Miriam and Aaron!

David

In Psalms 68:31(Leadership Bible, NIV) David declared in the midst of a National Celebration that the Nations in the entire world would soon learn about the Lord and come to worship Him. Psalm 68 became a Prophetic Word that Africa would have the opportunity to hear and receive the Gospel of Jesus Christ and it came to pass!

When Phillip reached the Ethiopian in Acts 8, (Leadership Bible, NIV) it opened the door to Africa.

A military victory gave David a 'Name for Himself', but created hostility between Israel and one of its ethnic rivals. II Samuel 8:13-14 (Leadership Bible, NIV) tells the story. David made a name for himself in what was called the 'Valley of Salt'. It was a wasteland close to the Dead Sea. David's exploits made him great, but were coming back to haunt Solomon. He earned his great name at the expense of 18,000 Syrians, people of Edom. God had specifically commanded His people not to 'Abhor' the Edomites because they were descendants of Jacob.

Yet Joab, David's general, continues battle until he slew every male in Edom. The Israelites hated the Edomites, so they were happy! They had adopted an attitude of 'Prejudice' because they were hurt.

A young boy named Hadad watched the slaughter before his father's servant could escape with him to Egypt. He never forgot what he saw. Then several years later after David dies, and Solomon turned away from God, God allowed Hadad to return to Palestine. There he became a royal thorn in the side of Solomon.

Solomon's life was affected by the brutal attitude of ethnic policies between David and Joab. David made a name for himself, but he did it at the expense of someone else' life and reputation. This is a tragic fruit of racism. The Church cannot allow this to happen. The Millennium Church will be that type Church that will forbid such behavior, or refuse to tolerate it!

Rev. Mrs. Kathy Sandlin

Solomon

Solomon built a beautiful temple in Jerusalem that was intended to be a "House of Prayer For All Nations" (I Kings 8:41-43, Living Bible, NIV). As Solomon's Prayer of Dedication for the Temple at Jerusalem, he showed that The God of Israel was a God for all nations. As king, he anticipated that foreigners from all over the world would have a desire to come to this House of Worship. So he asked The Lord to honor their prayers in order that "all peoples of the earth may know your Name and fear You."

Solomon received an early answer to his prayer when paid a visit by the Queen of Sheba in I Kings 10 (Leadership Bible, NIV). She had heard of the splendor of his kingdom, but she wanted to see them for herself. After she saw all of his accomplishments, she praised God for all of the things that He had done in Jerusalem!

Even though the temple was located inside Jerusalem, Jesus pointed out that this was to be a "House of Prayer For All Nations." (Leadership Bible, NIV). Jesus included all people in His life and Ministry. He never left anyone out, regardless of race, color, creed or gender.

Not only did Solomon include people from all walks of life and all races, he also married women from a number of different ethnic groups. The Shulamite in The Song of Solomon was among them. The groom, preferable Solomon, was described to be "white and ruddy (Sol 5:10, Leadership Bible, NIV) while the bride is dark, like the black tents of Kedar. If these descriptions depict skin color, then Solomon was certainly marrying a woman from a different ethnic background. This indicated that she might be Arabian or African.

Marriages across ethnic and racial lines in the ancient world were not uncommon. Yet today, they pose a problem for some people. No matter what reasons people may have for opposing interracial unions, The Bible neither condemns them nor prohibits them. The Israelites were forbidden to marry Canaanites, Ammonites, or Moabites. These prohibitions were not based upon mere ethnicity, but had to do with religion, morality, and geo-political considerations.

God created all of the races upon this earth. Differences in background and skin color may be hard for people to accept, but not for God. He reached out to all the world. "For God so loved the world that He gave His only begotten Son that whosoever believeth in Him should not perish, but have everlasting life." (John 3:16, Leadership Bible, NIV).

Isaiah

As far as Isaiah was concerned God is an International God. Isaiah considered Him to be The Lord of all the Nations. As He prayed in the temple, Isaiah saw himself, he saw The Lord and he saw the world.

Jeremiah

Jeremiah's life was saved by a quick-thinking Ethiopian who intervened with the plans of a king on behalf of the prophet.

The Millennium Church will be congregations of people that will not have hang ups for past traditions of other churches. Some churches will never be able to accept Multiethnic groups nor Intercultural Ministry. The Millennium Church will have no problem both accepting and ministering to these people in the last days just before Jesus comes.

Ethnic Walls Begin to Crumble

In Acts Chapter 10 (Leadership Bible, NIV), we see a major breakthrough in Racial Relationships. A wall had been erected between the Jews and Gentiles and for years had been a stumbling block to The Apostles. The wall of Racism had prevented them from having, and sharing Jesus in order to reverse the atmosphere.

In Acts Chapter 10 (Leadership Bible, NIV), a major breakthrough in racial relations begins to take place. For years there had been a wall between the Jews and the Gentiles that had kept The Apostles from ever being able to share Jesus with the Gentiles. Then finally, Peter met Cornelius, and there were two conversions that actually took place. Cornelius, his family, and his friends all accepted Christ. At the same time, Peter realized that God wanted Gentiles in the church.

One of the greatest hurdles of the church at this point was the cultural walls around Judaism. God needed a particular type of leader to play a specific role. It was not very likely that Gentiles would ever be accepted by a Jewish church unless God moved strategically. Peter was an unschooled man from Galilee. But God saw that Cornelius and Peter together could bring about a crumbling of the walls of racism. Cornelius' qualifications, along with Peter and his anointing, were God's men for the job. Cornelius had an impeccable character and had earned the respect of both the Jews and Gentiles in his community. He was a tough man, yet tender. He was loved, respected, approachable, powerful, a caring friend, and at the same time, a no-nonsense leader.

Cornelius was a Centurion in an Italian Regiment. Which meant he would have the image of tough, ruthless, commanding, and authoritative. He was a battle-hardened leader of the world's toughest soldiers, yet he was a tender, loving family man that prayed with his wife and children on a daily basis. Cornelius was a man of humility. He invited Peter to his home knowing that he was a Jew. Peter was comparable to a cultural inferior to Cornelius, yet when Peter entered his home, this military leader "met him and fell at his feet in reverence." As soon as Peter and Cornelius had completed their meeting, the first Gentile church was born!

To break down ethnic walls is a tough job for any leader. That is why it must be someone who is somewhat Apostolic and flexible. This is a strategic task. Cornelius could lead on a battlefield as well as in a general prayer meeting, hold the respect of the Gentile soldiers and the Jewish citizens, train his regiment and still give his family their necessary attention and spiritual leadership. Cornelius was handpicked by God for the task of not only being instrumental in tearing down these walls of prejudice, but at the same time, to teach Peter a very valuable lesson!

God's Synopsis of Cornelius

God saw Cornelius as a devout man. He viewed him as one who feared God and loved his family. God understood him to be very generous to the poor. He looked upon Cornelius as a man of prayers and alms that were received by God. He was also obedient to God's angel. He was cleansed by God and therefore was not to be considered unclean. God was trying to get across to Peter that because of the shed blood of Jesus Christ, this powerful centurion could be cleansed and accepted by God. It was unlawful for a Jewish man to keep company with or go to one of another nation. But something happened to Peter when God saved the household of Cornelius.

It broke down the walls inside of Peter's heart.

Peter's Concept of Cornelius

Peter had a different idea about Cornelius than God did. He saw him as a Centurion, which was a commander of 100 occupying Roman troops. He was a Gentile and Peter considered him to be unclean. It was unlawful for a Jew to visit a Gentile, being from another nation. Cornelius was also uncircumcised, which made him unholy to eat with. As far as Peter was concerned, all of these things disqualified Cornelius from serving him a meal, let alone being saved. Somehow, God intended to de-program Peter regarding a 'Jewish Gospel'!

Peter Receives A New Perspective

Several things happened to Peter as soon as God finished with him. One thing he concluded was that God shows no partiality. Secondly he learned that in every nation, whoever fears Him, accepts Him as Savior. He came to the conclusion that Jesus Christ is Lord of all, and whosoever receives Him will receive remission of their sins. "For as many as received Him, to them gave He power to become the sons of God." (Leadership Bible, NIV). Attitudes of prejudice and legalism are creating havoc in the church today. We must rid ourselves of attitude, pre-conceived ideas, or anything with Racial barriers in the church today. We must acquire a different mindset.

God Has Insight To Peter

God was ready to throw the door open to the Gentiles. However, Peter was deeply confused. God had sternly declared to Peter that what He had cleansed he was not allowed to call common or unclean. Because Jesus had paid the price on Calvary, now the Centurion could be cleansed from sin and become a son of God. So, what was Peter to do? Should he break his culture and befriend this Gentile?

Should he violate traditional codes he had been taught through the years? During his two-day journey to the home of Cornelius, he had an emotional struggle and voiced to the assembled crowd, "You know that it is not lawful for a Jewish man to keep company with or go to one from another nation." (Leadership Bible, NIV). However, God broke down the ethnic wall in Peter's heart by pouring out the Holy Spirit upon the Gentile believers.

The church must change her mind set. She cannot afford to wall herself off because of fear or prejudice. These are sensitive issues, but they must be addressed. The Millennium Church will be the caliber of people that will seek out people from all cultures. They will love them according to God's principles, and love them for the sake of the gospel. They will look at them from God's perspective. To turn away the Multiethnic/Multicultural groups of people from the church is to break the compassionate heart of God. Jesus said, "Whosoever will, may come!" (Leadership Bible, NIV). Aren't we glad?

Sheep Number 100

In John chapter 4 (Leadership Bible, NIV), we read the account of Jesus and the woman at the well. Jesus was never one to show partiality. He loves everyone the same. He spent His life upon the earth ministering to a pluralistic society. He treated all the same. He sat at a well and took the time to speak into the adulterous life of a woman who was bound for eternity with no hope of salvation. The scripture reveals to us that Jesus made the statement, "I must needs go through Samaria…" He always approached people on their own terms. To Him, every problem was important as well as unique. He was the perfect model of what it is like to live, work, communicate the message that He came to the earth to bring to people of all races, colors, creeds, and backgrounds.

Jesus was more interested in change than challenge in the lives of these unconverted people. He knew that if the change came, the challenge would be there. His prioritized interest was not so much where they came from, but where they were going as they departed this world. The Millennium Church will reflect a comparable approach to these type people whose lives have been shattered by sin and they are ready to build or build again. This Samaritan Woman is depicted in scripture as having five husbands, and living with one at their conversation that was not her husband. It was uncommon that the Jews had any dealings with the Samaritans. However, Jesus bypassed the law and the tradition in order to salvage a life that was headed for total destruction. He could have been stoned, lost His influence, had His disciples to leave Him, etc....but none of these things mattered above the salvation of this woman.

He poured into her one-on-one. There was not a mass crowd. She was sheep number 100. When she accepted Jesus as her Christ, she left her water pot at the well and ran into the city to tell the great things that Jesus had done for her. Because of this ethnic conversion, the entire city accepted Jesus Christ! The color of her skin did not temper her testimony. Her mixed ancestral heritage did not prohibit her from having a chance for eternal life as far as Jesus was concerned.

Because of what Christ did for her, she shared with those whom she knew that He could also love for who they were. She was instrumental in bringing an entire town to Jesus. Sheep number 100 is important, no matter what others may think say or do. The Millennium Church will be of such caliber, that race will not even enter their minds and there will be a constant inflow of people into their fellowships. Living water will only last so long, but Jacob's well is a supply that will never run dry! She was poor, but that never changed the mind of Jesus about her importance.

Nicodemus

We know Nicodemus in the scriptures as an upper class Jew, a Pharisee from one of the prominent families of Jerusalem. One night as he approached Jesus, He confronted him with his need to be born again. Afterward, Nicodemus went away for a while to think about the things that Jesus had said. Sometime later, we find this same upper class Jew defending Jesus on a procedural matter. However, He did not openly confess to know Jesus nor identify with Him until after Jesus was Crucified on Calvary. He and Joseph of Arimethea were the ones who took Jesus body off of the cross and prepared His body for burial.

The Samaritan Woman responded to Jesus instantly. Nicodemus took his time. Whether Jesus was speaking to a person with a scandalous lifestyle with five husbands, or whether He was addressing a rich upper class citizen, He gave everyone equal opportunity. Jesus was never prejudiced. Different people responded to Him in various ways, for the simple reason he dealt with them in various ways. Some came to Him after they were healed, fed, or taught. Many times they just responded to His miracles. The Millennium Church will reach out with arms of love to inherit those in the spirit who have been told that they have no inheritance in the things of God. They will be creative in the ways they present the Gospel in order that all who call upon the name of The Lord shall be saved. Why did Jesus never reflect the disease of prejudice? Because He was not a 'White-Man!'

Jesus was a dark – skinned Ethiopian Jew. Jesus was an intercontinental refugee. He was Asian Born. Then He fled to Africa with Mary and Joseph to avoid a political infanticide that was ordered by King Herod. He spent his formative years displaced from His own homeland. They finally migrated back to Palestine, and from there settled in Nazareth in rural Galilee. Jesus understood the pain of forced migration.

Rev. Mrs. Kathy Sandlin

In March 2001, the opportunity was afforded to my husband and I to take a mission trip to Brussels, Belgium. While ministering there, I had the privilege to preach to multitudes of Nationalities. The altar services were charged every night with the power of God. My Armor-Bearers were having a difficult time staying around me because the intensity of The Holy Spirit was so strong I was moving through the altars at a very rapid rate.

I took four Muslim men by the hand and led them to Jesus Christ. I laid hands on and preached to such Nationalities as Jews, Arabs, Muslims, Palestinians, Chinese, Portuguese, Japanese, Korean, American, Africans, Afghanistan's, Gypsies, Mexicans, Hispanics, Russians, Filipinos, Germans, Dutch, French, and on and on! I thought as I preached and prayed for all of these precious people, this is what it must have been like for Jesus as He traveled the globe and impacted the lives of people on a daily basis. He never limited Himself to one certain clique or group, He reached out and touched all who would hear and receive. I thank God everyday for that experience. It absolutely changed my life forever.

The Millennium Church will have the love of Jesus shed abroad in our hearts and not only reach, but reach to touch! New churches that are being started and planted must be Globally Envisioned people that will impact the world for the sake of the Kingdom of God!

CHAPTER 9

The Meticulous Church

The Word Meticulous means, "Extremely careful in attending to details...." I Peter 2:9 (Leadership Bible, NIV) gives forth an informative description of the Meticulous Church. "But ye are a chosen generation, a royal priesthood, a holy nation, a peculiar people, that you should show forth the praise of Him who has called you out of darkness, into His marvelous light; Which in times past were not a people, but are now the people of God, which had not obtained mercy."

The Church of The Millennium will be a people that will be very meticulous in all that they do. They will not be satisfied with a half-shod job. Whatsoever their hand finds to do they will be willing to do it with all of their might. This 21ˢᵗ Century will pursue a constant spirit of excellence in every facet of their ministry. Details will be at the priority head of the list,. There will be very little function in The Millennium Church that will bypass the eye and heart. There will be people that will be keenly Prophetic and will not only see, but know prophetically what is going on, and what is about to happen!

Chosen

The word 'Chosen' means, "To be selected from several; preferred." This chosen generation that Peter speaks about is among the very elect of God. They are chosen because of His foreknowledge. They have been born again to a lively hope! All of this means that God has called each one of them out of sin, to be a part of His redeemed people. As His redeemed people, we must stand out in the crowd! There is just something about us that is definitive among other people. We are the redeemed of The Lord! Let the redeemed of The Lord say so! It is comparable to having a family album. We know *who* we are because we know *whose* we are. All of these names that Peter calls believers are important to us because they reveal our identity. We belong to God. We have a call upon our lives from Him. It is The Grace of God that secures our identity and security.

Royalty

Secondly, The Millennium Church will have the appearance of Royalty. Royalty means "…a collection of royal persons…" Whenever we collect certain things, they are gathered over a period of time. The same is true with The Body of Christ! We are gathering the harvest now and getting ready for the Royal Banquet that will take place at the Marriage Supper of the Lamb. The Millennium Church will be busy gathering Harvest! They will not say wait four months and then see the harvest fields, they are aware that the fields are ripe and ready right now to be harvested. The Millennium Church will gather for church services. However, their church services will be much on the scale of Celebration Times. After they gather, they will scatter. Scatter to share the Gospel with all whom they come into contact with.

Then they will gather again to celebrate the harvest and the blessing of God upon their lives, bringing the first fruits of all that God has blessed them with! Royalty also means a people of dignity and power! *Meticulous! Sharp! Polished! Shining!* The Millennium Church will be a people of integrity. They will reflect the glory of God in their everyday lifestyle. It also means a character or quality proper to or befitting a sovereign example. "Arise, shine, for your light has come and the Glory of The Lord has risen upon thee..." (Isaiah 60:1, Leadership Bible, NIV).

Priesthood

The word priesthood means minister or someone who is ordained to perform religious rites and sacrificial offerings. A Royal Priesthood will be a collection of those who are ordained by God Himself and walk in a high realm of the spirit of The Lord. They will know that they are called by Him to carry out the work of the Ministry. In scripture, these believers were part of the fulfillment of God's plan to prepare a kingdom of priest for Himself. They were called to worship God not by offering animals as a sacrifice, but to present their own bodies as a living sacrifice, available for His purposes. (Romans 12:1, Leadership Bible, NIV) (Rev 1:6, Leadership Bible, NIV).

A Holy Nation

Leviticus declares to us, "Be ye holy, even as I also am Holy." God had called these people to Himself and therefore they were expected to be holy. (I Peter 1:16, Leadership Bible, NIV). Their lifestyles were to reflect the very character of God. Their identity as His people was to be expressed in their everyday character. The Millennium Church must be made up of a people with quality character, who will be enabled by The Holy Spirit to help new converts, as well as others within The Body, to develop a character reflecting the love of God and the fruit of The Spirit.

A Peculiar People

The word Peculiar in this scripture means to be Special! They were called to a special intimate relationship with God. Secret Places with God were mandatory. These fiery passionate places with God would be the territory that would spawn impregnation in the spiritual wombs of believers and then they would bring forth babies in the spirit. Not only would they have a unique relationship with God, but they were required by The Lord to have a sincere relationship with one another. By doing so, these people would have a unique relationship and access to Him as God. The Church of The Millennium will follow this special pattern for their access to God.

Before they speak their prayers, God will answer them. (Jeremiah 33:3) "Call unto me and I will answer thee and show thee great and mighty things which thou knowest not!" (Leadership Bible, NIV).

Called Into His Light

Peter reminded these believers of what it means to be a child of The Living God! The Millennium Church will be a people of Focus, meticulously focusing upon their standing with Christ. Christ is the Savior who called them out of their former lifestyle of darkness and brought them forth into the light of the glorious gospel. They were special people in the eyes of Jesus. The Millennium Church will be special to God and they will know just how special because of the blessings that will be poured out from heaven upon them.

Kingdom Personnel

This special 21st century church will have a different mindset when it comes to excellence in The Kingdom of God. The congregations of these churches will be made up of many different people from all walks of life. Some of these people will lack confidence in themselves, their significance and competence when it comes to being the children of the most high God. Self-doubt will sometimes be exemplified and therefore out of the abundance of the heart the mouth will speak. This Millennium Church will become instrumental in changing all of that.

Ministry will no longer just belong to church staff. The Biblical Principle regarding *Ministry* is that all believers have a responsibility to heed to the calling and gift of God within them.

Calling refers to not only those who are entering into a professional religious call, but it also has reference to God's invitation for all to come to the saving knowledge of Jesus Christ.

Laity and Lay People are not second-class citizens in the Body of Christ. All Christians are fully equipped by God to accomplish the work of the ministry.

(Romans 12:6; I Cor. 12:7; Ephesians 4:12; I Peter 4:10-11; Leadership Bible, NIV).

The Millennium Church will be a people who make up Kingdom Personnel. They will be trained and equipped to do the work the ministry with excellence. They will pay special attention to the things in The Kingdom of God that matter the most. They will not be drawn aside by petty things. They will be keen and alert to the little foxes that spoil the vine. They will be so busy upon the wall, they will refuse to come down and break the focus of what they are doing.

Things like carpet color, painting the church, paving the parking lot, who steps into what position, declaring numbers for the sake of numbers, etc….will not be their priority nor focus. These things are definitely important, but will not be first and foremost.

The Leadership of this New Breed of church will focus on more important things such as, "How Many people accepted Christ in our services today? Who received the Baptism of The Holy Spirit in the services? What is The Spiritual temperature of our church body? Is it hot, cold, or lukewarm? Are the sermons that I am preaching fresh bread from Heaven? Or are they cold and stale? How many people were healed in the altar service this past Sunday? Are these people paying tithe to The Lord? Are we growing the church, or are we growing the people?"

These are the types of things that the leaders and laity of The Millennium Church will be made up of. Meticulous in all-important areas. Extremely careful to attend to details. This church is A Chosen Generation, A Royal Priesthood, A Holy Nation, A Peculiar People called out of darkness into His marvelous light! This body of born again believers will be free of heavy weight bondages that have kept people from growing in The Lord. They will be filled with excitement as they pursue God, their relationship with Him, and minister with excellence!

The Meticulous Millennium Church will be a very unique group of Worshippers.

CHAPTER 10

The Miraculous Church

Acts 19:11 ".....And God wrought special miracles by the hands of Paul...."(Leadership Bible, NIV).

The word *miraculous* means, "An extra ordinary event as a sign of Divine intervention in human affairs; a marvel...."

I remember as a little girl growing up in a Full Gospel church, that there seemed to be a lot of emphasis put upon the miraculous. In fact, the international movement where I was raised was built upon the manifestation of miracles. The people believed in signs and wonders and the supernatural power of God. Miracles were a faith issue. Now days, every miracle performed by God seems to have to go through and analyzing process. By doing such, we inevitably dilute the power of God and literally strangle the life out of our church services. In return for all of that, we literally launch a platform for the crushing of the faith of people.

The Millennium Church must operate in the miraculous. Miracles are not a thing of the past. They are performed by the God of today. The same God whom performed miracles yesterday said, "Jesus

Christ, the same yesterday, today and forever!" (Leadership Bible, NIV). He does not change; we are the ones who change. The caliber of The Millennium Church will be such that it will be able to offer people in the world a God answer to their problems. Society of this day is made up of a collage of people whose lives are in ruins over some bad choices, uncontrollable circumstances, or just the mere situations of life.

We have churches that are filled with people who are saved, yet they are a saved mess! They require spiritual uplift, by pouring in the oil and helping them to become established. Many struggle with problems of various sorts. Some are bound by such things as drugs, alcohol, perversion, greed, power, fear, and anxiety. These types of people need help from God and the church. Jesus made this declaration plainly to His disciples. "The works that I do shall you do, and greater works shall you do!" What a powerful command and promise!

Much of our church structures today remain very skeptical about what takes place in the church world. They mock at the signs and the wonders. They make fun of those who minister and those who receive. They scoff at the Scriptures, laugh whenever someone is blessed, and have very little desire to see salvation come to someone. Much of this type behavior stems from a jealousy factor within them. People of this sort will rejoice over anything as long as they receive the credit for what is being done or if they look good in the eyes of people during the process.

Miracles Require Faith

Miracles are supernatural divine interventions by God and are only released where there is a supernatural level of faith. A lack of faith produces a lack of miracles. Jesus said that if we only had faith as a grain of mustard see we could remove mountains and cast them into the Sea! *The Millennium Church will be required by God to possess and not just profess.* This church will know that is should not make statements with the mouth that the heart cannot back up. It will be composed of a people of maturity in the things of God. There will be balance in their spiritual appetite. They will eat the meat of The Word and not just drink the milk of The Word. The meat of all that God has to say will enable them to be strong and carry out the divine mandate of God upon their lives, churches, and communities. They will understand the importance of exercising their spiritual muscles; therefore, they will grow and mature.

As Jesus ministered on the earth, one of His favorite subjects was faith. Why? Faith produces the natural impossibilities in life! He not only preached about faith; He practiced and then demonstrated the power of faith. The woman with the issue of blood, as she touched the hem of the garment of Jesus, was miraculously healed. He quickly responded to her and said, "Daughter, be of good cheer; *your faith* has made you well. Go in peace." (Leadership Bible, NIV).

Prophetic Instructors

The Millennium Church will not just teach and preach that people can be healed, but will give forth prophetic instruction on *HOW* to be healed. Its members will know how to walk those in need through a Scriptural process and help them to find their pathway to total healing. We can and should believe God for miracles, but there are certain guidelines and boundaries that we should operate in so that healing can come forth for us. For instance, if we have high blood pressure, then we know that there are certain things that should not be eaten, so we should eliminate them from our diet. If there are particular settings of circumstances that cause us emotional upset, then either conquer them or stay away from them. If we have diabetes, don't eat sugar! These are just examples to help you better understand what I mean by prophetic instructors. They will discern and then apply both Biblical and Natural wisdom to bring remedy to the situation.

Word of Knowledge

The Millennium Church will be comprised of people who operate in the gifts of The Holy Spirit on new and different levels. Even as they pray for people, The Holy Spirit will begin to reveal sicknesses, disease, and chronic illnesses; and they will be able to accurately pinpoint them and pray targeted intercession over these things. As they pray, God will manifest Himself dynamically for the total eradication of these things from the body.

Shadow Casters

Then, last but not least, there will be those who are anointed to pray and see the miraculous manifestations of The Holy Spirit. They will be called, 'Shadow Casters'. *Acts 5:14-16 says, "And believers were continually added to the Lord, both men and women, so that they brought the sick out into the streets and laid them on beds and couches, that at least the 'Shadow Of Peter passing by might fall on some of them. Also a multitude gathered from the surrounding cities to Jerusalem, bringing sick people and those who were tormented by unclean spirits, and they were healed."(Leadership Bible, NIV).*

I believe in these last days that we will see people healed on the streets, and in places like restaurants, shopping centers, malls, and school systems. Even as people walk by them, I believe that the anointing of The Holy Ghost will be so strong upon us, as members of this last day church, that people in our midst can and will receive their instantaneous healing. I can see prophetically people will be brought to the parking lots and sidewalks of our churches desperate for God and desperate for their miracle. I believe our very shadow can heal them! They will even make their way to our workplaces in desperation for the touch of God! This Millennium Church will be made of people with the anointing for the working of miracles.

Acts 3 (Leadership Bible, NIV) gives us a description also, of the miraculous healing at the temple at the hour of prayer. Peter and John were being looked upon for a miracle. The Scripture says the lame man was looking upon Peter and John, *expecting* to receive something of them. The Millennium Church will be looked upon because it will be such a uniquely powerful people, but also those looking will look for and see God Himself in their midst. They will expect something from us as this church!

In Acts 19:11 (Leadership Bible, NIV), God worked unusual miracles by the hands of Paul, so much to the degree of miraculous that the handkerchiefs and aprons were brought from his body to the sick and they were healed. Evil spirits were also cast out of them. That is the kind of power with which this last day church will operate and in which this church will operate. We will speak in the name of Jesus and these things will have to go! Whether we are wearing aprons, handkerchiefs, or just walking down the street, the power of The Holy Spirit will be at work and "sitting on ready" in our lives! The Millennium Church will most definitely be a miraculous church!

From The Pulpit To The Pew

Even as The Word of God is preached from the pulpit, I believe there will be people who will be healed in their seats. There will not have to be the laying on of hands for these miracles to happen. The Power of God will be strong inside of These Millennium Churches; nothing will have to be stirred up nor orchestrated by man. Also, we need to keep in mind that the works of man in this type of church will not manipulate The Holy Spirit. In order to have this type of miraculous working of The Holy Spirit, we must understand that The Holy Spirit will require of us to let Him be the center of attention and the point of attraction! Do not misunderstand what I say to you. The Millennium Church services may be structured, planned, and made ready by man; but God Himself must order these types of services.

In any event, there must be focus, not on the miracle, but the Miracle Worker. In the Book of Acts, miracles, signs, and wonders, always followed the preaching, confirming Word of God. Miracles today still follow the preaching of The Word. In the Synoptic Gospels, the miracles performed were not just healings. They consisted of things such as deliverances, exorcisms, financial provision, safety interventions, and the raising of the dead.

God will use the faith and preparations of The Millennium Church to cause miracles to happen. But these miracles will not take place unless God receives all of the glory for what is being done. God will perform them for the purpose of drawing people to Jesus Christ. As Peter and John walked into the temple that day and the lame man was healed that had been crippled from his birth, thousands of people were saved as this miracle alone gave Peter a platform to declare the Gospel. It brought repentance to the crowd that was drawn to Solomon's Porch!

When Jesus raised Lazarus from the dead, He prayed a prayer that said, "Father, I do not ask you to do this for me, but for the sake of all of these people who are standing around this tomb." (Leadership Bible, NIV). He wanted the people who were watching to know that this miracle was nothing short of the power of God, and He wanted His Father to receive all of the Glory for the miracle!

This kind of miracle will require an expensive price. That price is intercession and Bible study. It will also require a set order of fasting and prayer among not just the leadership of these type churches, but it will also be required of the laity. There are some things that just do not come forth except by prayer and fasting! I am excited to know that God is bringing forth a new breed of people that will be one of the most powerful churches among others in the earth.

The Millennium Church will be one of its kind, yet it will have the potential to *reproduce*!

Mark, chapter 16 says, "And these signs shall follow them that believe. In My Name they will cast out demons; they will speak with new tongues; they will take up serpents; and if they drink any deadly thing, it will by no means hurt them; they will lay hands on the sick, and they shall recover." (Leadership Bible, NIV). This is a full description of The Millennium, Miraculous Church! We have a *kairos* time to fill all of the earth with the knowledge and the glory of an Almighty God!

CHAPTER 11

The Multiplication Church

In the Book of Genesis, God spoke to Adam and Eve and said to them, "Be ye fruitful, and *MULTIPLY*! Fill the earth and subdue it; have dominion over every living thing that moves upon the face of the earth!" (Leadership Bible, NIV). It has been the very heart of God from the beginning of creation that all that he created be blessed and experience INCREASE! He has His own investment system set in place for His people to prosper. However, there are also stipulations to His blessing our efforts. We must release what God has put into our hands, so that He can release what He has in His!

We must remember that God created The Universe. The very first of the Scriptures refer to God as a *WORKER*! He worked six days and the seventh day He rested. We also must remember that we are created in His image. Therefore, we must also be workers. Everything that our hands find to do, we must do it with all of our might! God is not lazy. God may at times seem to be silent, but God is never still! God is honored in His work, in that He replied, "It is Good!" (Leadership Bible, NIV). The Millennium Church will need this same intent 'workers personality' in order to bring about multiplication and honor of God.

Good Stewardship

From the very time that God created Adam and Eve, He expected stewardship of them. A steward manages the possessions of another. We are all stewards of the resources, abilities, and opportunities that God has entrusted to our care, and we will one day give an account of how we have used them. If God has trusted us, then we must prove ourselves faithful with what He has placed into our hands. The Millennium Church must have a 'stewardship mentality' in order to attain the trust of God more and more! If we are faithful in the little things, Jesus promised that we would become ruler over big things!

Redemptive Lift

I believe that God operates His kingdom somewhat by a system of 'redemptive lift.' For instance, if I live in a four room, run down home, and I want my next home to be something of greater value, then I must take care of it to the best of my ability. I must pay my rent, lease, or house payment faithfully. If I pay tithe and offering to God, taking care of His Kingdom first; then, I believe that God implements redemptive lift in my life and will consistently give me increase on all He has given me. I have the potential to have a mansion if I am faithful with what God has put into my hands. I may drive a beat up paint ridden, ugly car, but if I take care of it, and give God what is His, I have the potential to drive a Mercedes one day!

Reproduction

By sowing and giving back to God what is His, I am opening the pathway very clearly for return upon my investments! When I sow seed, that seed has the potential to reproduce. I am not just talking about financial seed; I am talking about everything that I sow. God spoke to me a few days ago and said, "If you will sow something every day, then you will reap something every day." That excited me. I have looked for places to sow and reproduce by potential. If we give a cup of cold water in His name, we will not lose our reward! There are three laws to harvest. First of all, we reap what we sow; Secondly, we reap more than we sow; and Thirdly, we reap later than we sow.

The Millennium Church is called to be a Matthew 25 church (Leadership Bible, NIV). It will actually go forth and look for the right places to sow that it may reap. It will be known as a church of multiplication. Its members will consistently experience increase in their lives, jobs, homes, families, health, finances, and church! These people who will make up The Millennium Church will walk in expectancy and be a noticeably blessed people of God as they receive His outpouring of abundance upon their lives.

They will hunger to walk in the wisdom of God and to use wisely what the Lord has released to them. They will be blessed in the city and blessed in the field. They will be the head and not the tail – the lender and not the borrower. They will be fruitful and multiply across the earth. The Millennium Church body will have houses that they did not build; vineyards they did not plant. The Word of God declares these things to us and I believe and receive them in the Name of Jesus.

Churches Will Multiply

Churches of The Millennium will not just add to their congregations' daily. They will be fruitful and multiply! This church will be a replica of The New Testament Churches that we read about in the Book of Acts. I believe that we will even see greater works than these as Jesus so told His disciples! The churches in the Book of Acts were not churches comparable to what we have today. They were started in the streets and carried on in the streets. They were small crowds at first, and they multiplied as the Apostle carried out the commandments of Jesus. The home and living quarters housed these mighty movements. There were also strategic places that The Holy Spirit would implement miracles and draw multitudes of people in order for The Gospel to be preached.

Acts Chapter 6 (Leadership Bible, NIV) reflects a powerful story to us of how the 'Word of God spread and the number of the disciples multiplied in Jerusalem, and a great many of the priest were obedient to the faith.' We also read about a man named Stephen. Stephen was not an Apostle, yet he was a mighty man in God, full of faith and full of power, doing miracles, signs and wonders among the people. There were a few disputers, but they were not able to resist the spirit and the wisdom with which Stephen spoke.

We must remember that in order to build the church, we must first build people. Whether it was just one person, ten people, or a vast crowd, the Apostles were spreading The Word of God and the churches were being planted and growing everywhere. Acts Chapter six is the first of several accounts given of the churches that were growing and being multiplied.

Comfort Brings Multiplication

Acts 9:31 reads *"Then the churches throughout all Judea, Galilee, and Samaria had peace and were edified. And walking in the fear of the Lord and in the comfort of the Holy Spirit, they were multiplied."* (Leadership Bible, NIV). The church here begins to prosper as they rest in the Holy Ghost. They knew because of their relationship with the Lord and the call upon their lives that they were going to see the church grow and prosper. The Bible says, "Except The Lord build the house, they labor in vain who build it." When the church begins to understand that, 'It is not by might, nor by power, but by my spirit says the Lord,'(Leadership Bible, NIV) it is then that we will experience the growth in the church that we desire to see. The Apostles were comforted in knowing they were just an instrument and that God was in control.

The word comfort in this scripture means, a calling alongside to help, to comfort, to give consolation or encouragement; a strengthening presence; one who upholds those who are appealing for assistance. The Apostles knew that as they walked before The Lord in His presence the work would happen. They did not worry or fret. They knew the promises of God that were "Yea and Amen!"

The Generation Of 'Herods'

The family line of Herod, symbolizes the acts of Satan against the church to destroy it. Herod The Great launched an attack to kill Jesus; his son beheaded John the Baptist; his grandson beheaded James and was hiding Peter so that he could also execute him. In Acts Chapter 12, the people of Tyre and Sidon asked that their country have peace. Herod gathered them together in the city streets to speak to them. They began to cry out for peace and gave glory to God. When Herod refused to give God glory, the worms came and ate him and he died! Acts 12:24, "But the Word of God grew and multiplied." (Leadership Bible, NIV). The Herod's of this day will not plague The Millennium Church. Its prayer and intercession will allow The Lord to be a shield about the members and the glory seekers will not be able to rob God of the Glory that is due unto Him.

The Word of God will multiply and spread, as These Millennium Churches understand more and more that the church belongs to God. Therefore, no weapon formed against her shall prosper!

Mentoring Brings Multiplication

In Acts Chapter 15 (Leadership Bible, NIV), contention rose between Paul and Barnabas. They separated: Barnabas took John Mark, Paul took Silas, and they went their separate ways to minister. In Acts 16, (Leadership Bible, NIV) Paul and Silas came to Derbe and Lystra. There was a young man there named Timothy. He was a member of the local church at Lystra and had a good recommendation from the people there and at Iconium. Paul felt prompted by The Holy Spirit to bring Timothy alongside and to mentor and train him in the faith. He was now a member of Paul's apostolic team, and they traveled on to declare The Gospel. Paul later placed Timothy in charge of the church in Ephesus and the sound Biblical wisdom and knowledge of Paul that was imparted into Timothy became a foundation for example in Apostolic faith. Timothy became a powerful pastor and the church grew and multiplied because Paul took the time to mentor Timothy.

We all have the power to reproduce ourselves into someone else. What God has invested in us through our spiritual growth, we can multiply by depositing that into someone else who has the same gifts, calling, anointing or even potential as we do. Mentoring brings forth multiplication.

Miracles Bring Multiplication

In Acts Chapter 19, (Leadership Bible, NIV) as God was working special miracles by the hands of Paul, multiplication was happening with The Word of God and with the churches. The miracles of the aprons and handkerchiefs of Paul were bringing magnification to Jesus Christ in the city! Diseases and evil spirits were taking their flight as Paul laid hands on them and they were instantaneously set free!

There were some Jewish exorcists who tried to cast out devils, as well as the seven sons of Sceva, who was a Jewish chief priest. The evil spirit replied, "Jesus I know, and Paul I know, but who are you?" (Hebrew/Greek Key Study Bible). Then the man that the spirit was in leaped on them and overpowered and prevailed against them. They ran away naked and wounded. When all of the Jews and Greeks in Ephesus heard about this, they became afraid and the name of Jesus was magnified.

Those who practice witchcraft, magic, and occults brought their books together and burned them. The total cost of the books alone was estimated at fifty thousand pieces of silver. After that, the Word of God *GREW* and prevailed mightily!

Multiplication Mentality

The Millennium Church body of believers will have a multiplication mentality. They will have a vision to give birth to daughter churches. When couples unite in marriage, most of the time they make plans for children sometime in the future. The Millennium Church will make plans for their babies in the beginning stages of the mother church. They will set aside the necessary means for this to happen. Some will have multiple births because of the fertility of the womb of the church. The beautiful part of this is the mother church has the potential to be as fertile as she desires to be. She will control that fertility because of the level of relationship that she will have with The Lord.

She may give birth to one daughter or multiple daughters. The choice will be hers! If we are going to reach the population of the world for Jesus Christ, then we must operate in The Body of Christ with a multiplication mentality. That is the only way that we can reach them. We must multiply. Multiplication means growth and development. Just as God commanded Adam and Eve in the beginning, "Be Ye Fruitful And Multiply!" (Leadership Bible, NIV). That is true for the church today. We must "Go ye therefore and preach the Gospel to all nations." (Leadership Bible, NIV). Missions will be a part of this multiplication process.

We must start at home in Jerusalem. Then we can expand the borders and reach those in Judea, just a little further away. We take another step toward Samaria, the outer boundaries of our comfort zone. Then finally, we must go to the "uttermost parts of the earth." (Leadership Bible, NIV). Whether it is in our back door or whether we are across the ocean, The Word of God must grow and multiply. Churches must grow and multiply. The Millennium Church will have this mentality, not just in their minds, but also in their hearts!

CHAPTER 12

The Maiden Church

Finally, The Millennium Church will have attributes of a maiden church. Throughout all of my life, I have heard sermon after sermon, story after story about the second coming of Christ, and about how He would be returning to the earth one day to receive His bride. Many times, I have heard ministers refer to the church as His bride. I personally believe that the Bride will be chosen out of the Church. The Scriptures tell us that He is coming back for a Bride that is without spot, wrinkle, or blemish. He is looking for a virgin bride. One that is pure and holy. The church today is filled with many folks who think that they are ready for the rapture or the Second Coming of Christ, but they are fooling themselves.

They do and say all of the right things on the outward. However, on the inside, they are ravenous wolves. *They have pulpit and pew performance, but there is a lack of power in their lives to validate what they say and do.* There is a lack of relationship with the Father that produces a spiritual breach. *It is our prayer and intercession relationship with God that prepares us for everything that God has in store for our future.* Faith may move a mountain, but prayer will move God!

The Millennium Church will have a clear understanding of the importance of its relationship with The Lord. It is imperative that our churches begin to put into practice the basics and foundations of intercession in order to reach our full potential in The Lord. Jesus said in John Chapter 15, "Apart from me, you can do nothing." (Leadership Bible, NIV). Every ministry, every church service, every campaign, everything that we may endeavor to do for The Lord must have a foundation of intercession and be laced with compassionate prayer. Otherwise, she will not be prepared to meet the bridegroom!

This Millennium Maiden Church will have a desire for a passionate involvement with the bridegroom. Intense intercession will permeate both the heart of the church and the heart of God. There will be a unique heart connection between the two. They will long for the times that may come together for communion and not just communication. This relationship will build day-by-day as their betrothal paves the pathway for that special wedding day. The day that the bridegroom and the bride consummate their marriage and become as one! This Maiden Church will know how to please the bridegroom in every way. She will open her heart to Him and He to her. In doing so, their relationship will become more and more passionate and valuable to each other.

Her heart cry will be that of the psalmist David as he said, "Search me and know me; try me and see if there be some wicked way in me." (Leadership Bible, NIV). The purity of This Maiden Church will shine like the noonday sun. There will be no mistaking who she belongs to. Her wedding garments will be white as snow. There will be no spots, wrinkles nor blemishes upon her in any fashion. The time that the will share on earth will be just a small portion of what eternity will be like for them.

The Esther Anointing

A good example of The Millennium Maiden Church is Queen Esther. She was a beautiful young lady whom The Lord had set aside for a particular timely purpose. She was a seasonal representative of the love and liberating power of God – chosen for a "kairos" time. The Millennium Maiden Church is being raised up for a "kairos" time. Times of seasons and opportunities will be afforded to these type churches for the last days. Esther was full of compassion and intended to help her people even if it meant giving her life. Jesus said, "You have not chosen me, but I have chosen you and ordained you that you might bring forth fruit." (Leadership Bible, NIV). Such was the case with Queen Esther. She was both chosen and ordained.

The name *Esther* means 'Star'. This very book, The Millennium Church, is based upon Isaiah 60:1, "Arise, shine, for your light has come and the glory of the Lord has risen upon thee…." (Leadership Bible, NIV). Esther was a Jewish queen who was instrumental in saving her people from genocide by boldly speaking before the King and exposing the enemy and his plot to destroy them.

Preparation To Meet The King

After Queen Vashti had so blatantly refused to parade her beauty before her husband at his seven-day drinking festival, he disposed of her by a royal decree. She could no longer be allowed to come before the King. The King then appointed officers to gather all of the beautiful VIRGINS to the women's quarters. They were given beauty preparations to adorn themselves for a period of time, and then the King would choose which one he wanted for his own. As she was in a time of preparation, she found out that Mordecai was mourning in sackcloth and ashes and wanted to know more about the reason why! He sent her word that she had been brought to the

Kingdom for such a time as this and she pursued Mordecai's request. There is a time for adorning yourself and making sure that all things are in order. God is looking for a radiant Bride – one that shines with His glory. The Millennium Church will take the time to adorn herself, knowing that she must come daily into the presence of the King of Kings.

Preparation To Speak To The King

She and her MAIDENS fasted for three days and she made entrance to the king, for he was willing to give her his attention. The third day, Esther put on her royal robes and stood in the inner court of the King's Palace. As she stood in the inner court, she found favor in the sight of the King! He held out his golden scepter, giving her approval for entrance into him. When the King asked her for her request, he was ready to give her up to half of the Kingdom! Why the favor? How did all of this come about? Esther took the time on a daily basis for several months, to adorn herself. Her radiant beauty captivated an audience with the King himself!

We must begin to understand that we are children of the King. There is nothing shabby about a king; therefore as we come into the presence of our King, we must begin to approach Him with large expectation, Esther walked into the presence of the King with favor and acceptance. The Millennium Church must learn to do the same thing. Her willingness to prepare herself to go before the King saved the lives of her family and the lives of many others.

The Millennium Church will be a definite House of Prayer for All Nations! It will ignite the fire of intercession and the members will know when something is not in place or adorned. They will also make preparation to speak to the King on behalf of others. Their families will receive more prayer over them than ever before. The

Church itself will be saturated by intercessors whom God will assign to the church. God is doing a beautiful thing in assigning people to their posts of duty with The Millennium Church. The leadership of these churches will need consistent prayer covering. There will be extremely heavy pressure on these churches and leaders of this last day.

Breakthrough!

It is time for this church to begin to shine forth as the 'Star' or the Esther Anointed Fellowship. As she found favor with the King, he granted her to ask for anything that she so desire and he would give it to her up to half of the Kingdom! Breakthrough! All because she prepared herself to go into His presence as she did, he held out the golden scepter to her. She was his chosen bride. He could have had any princess that he may have wanted, but he chose her from a multitude of maidens. God answered her prayer and protected her heritage and her nation. We must have this type intercession over and around This Maiden Church in order for her to accomplish her purpose upon this earth. We must have instant access to the King and the throne room of grace. For Esther, the enemy was destroyed right before her very eyes. No weapon formed against her shall prosper! Hallelujah! The root of the attribute that won the battle for Esther was her favor with the King. Favor comes by relationship with the Father, knowing when to speak and what to say. We must have ears to hear what the spirit is saying unto the church today! She began in the role of a 'Maiden', and later become the Bride of the King! What a church!

Mary, The Mother of Jesus

The name Mary is also known as Miriam (of Nazareth); the Virgin. Mary was married to Joseph, Jesus' earthly father, and was the mother of four other sons, James, Joses, Judas, and Simon. Mary and Joseph also had daughters. She was a homemaker and a relative of Elizabeth, mother of John the Baptist. When Mary is informed that she will be the mother of the Messiah, she is taken back just a little. The Scriptures tell us that she was visited by the angel Gabriel to inform her of the news. The Scriptures also tell us that she was betrothed to a man named Joseph.

Betrothal

Betrothal was a mutual promise or a contract for a future marriage. The husband selected the bride; then there was a contract negotiated by a friend or agent representing the bridegroom, and by the parents representing the bride. It was always confirmed by an oath and presents were brought to the bride and her parents.

Betrothal was at that time celebrated by a feast. In some cases, it was all right for the bridegroom to place a ring upon the finger of the bride as a token of love and fidelity. In the Hebrew custom, betrothal was actually a part of the marriage process. Betrothal was much more closely linked with marriage process. If either party changed his or her mind, it became a serious matter, and could have been subject to a fine. Betrothal was much more closely linked with marriage than engagements that we experience today. However, the actual marriage took place when the bridegroom could take his bride to his home, and there the marriage was consummated by the sexual union.

This is step by step the same relationship between Christ and His church. We are betrothed to Him. He will one day step out on the clouds and make the selection of His bride. The contract has been negotiated by His agent, The Holy Spirit, and has been confirmed by the vows of His bride. She has been saturated by presents given by the Holy Spirit, and they have been put to use very well.

This betrothal is being celebrated by a feast even now, as we know that The Father has a table spread where the saints of God are fed. We are all invited to the table of The Lord and we have the opportunity to sit in His presence and partake of His table that He has spread before us.

The Bridegroom has placed a ring upon the finger of the Bride and they are now in covenant relationship one with another. Hallelujah!

We eagerly wait for that great and notable day when the trumpet shall sound and we find ourselves sailing through the air to ever be with Him. We will meet Him in the clouds with no hesitation. As His bride, He will be awestruck by the virginity and the beauty of her adornment, and the marriage is about to be consummated. For in our Father's House are many mansions. He has gone to prepare a place for her, and He promised that if he went away He would surely come again to receive us unto Himself, that where he is, there we may be also. The Millennium Church will be a Church that will have an ear to hear and will be ready when they hear His voice say, "All things are now made ready. The Spirit and the Bride say, Come!" (Leadership Bible, NIV).

The Handmaiden of The Lord

The word *handmaiden* literally means 'maidservant'. As soon as the Angel Gabriel finished with his address from The Lord, Mary responded by saying, "Behold the maidservant of The Lord. Let it be to me according to your word!" Mary found herself in a place of total submission to the will of God for her life. That is not always an easy place to acquire. To get there, flesh has to die. We must crucify our wants and desires in order to sometimes follow Christ fully.

When the angel came to Mary, she was no more than fifteen years of age. His announcement actually meant that this was the end of her 'normal life!' She could have caused gossip, rumor-mongers; Joseph could have decided to end the engagement through a divorce. He could have put her away secretly, but still she would have been alone and would have had to return to her father's home, or survive upon her own!

Mary had done nothing to cause this; neither had she pursued anything to have this happen. She could have refused to receive Gabriel's message, but instead she said, "Let it be to me according to your word." (Leadership Bible, NIV). She clearly submitted to the angel's message. She submissively accepted her assignment. The word *handmaiden* means, 'What can I do for you? Here I am!' That will be the heart cry of The Millennium Church. Be it unto me according to thy word. She was willing to lay her reputation on the line to obey The Father's will.

The Father's will for her was very clearly revealed. The Millennium Church will see immediately and know that 'This Is The Lord!' The word *maiden* means, "What can I do for you? Here I am. Whatever you desire of me, that will I do!"

The Millennium Church will need to be very alert and keenly awake to observe and do all that the Lord is putting into our hearts to do and accomplish! There are many things that await us for all of our ministries should Jesus tarry. As soon as Mary reached the home of

Elizabeth, she sang a song that says, "My Soul Doth Magnify The Lord!"

The Millennium Church must be like the maidens: Esther the Queen and Mary the mother of Jesus! We must adorn ourselves; we must prepare ourselves to go before the King. We must also be prepared to speak before the King. Then we must be willing to do what He says to us. Then we must be like Mary and say, "Let it be unto me according to thy word." (Leadership Bible, NIV).

Prayer, intercession, intense Bible study and the willingness to submit to The Father for His will to be accomplished will be keynote factors in The Millennium Church being prepared for the return of Christ. That church that is without spot, wrinkle, or blemish will be the one that he will take home with Him to consummate a marriage!

The Ten Virgins

In Matthew 25 (Leadership Bible, NIV), there were ten virgins. There were five wise and five foolish. The foolish waited until the midnight cry of the bridegroom and found themselves unprepared, with a lack of oil. The five wise virgins carried oil in their lamps and had extra oil just in case they needed it. They also took the time to regularly trim their wicks. The trimming of the wicks of these lamps signified that they were determined to keep their lamps burning brightly in order to light their path. This church must be careful to guard their oil – do not give it away. It is compared to the anointing of the Holy Spirit. This oil is far too precious and necessary for our use to run out. It must become, "….a lamp unto our feet and light unto our path." (Leadership Bible, NIV). For too many years, the church has done enough to just get by. As time goes on, I find that the requirements just to keep us with the commands of The Lord are very intense. The Bride must stay ready at all times. Jesus said, "In such an hour as you think not, the Son of Man will come. Watch therefore and be ready!"

Jesus will return for the virgins that will make up a spotless bride. He is looking for a Bride, not a date! He expects consistency from us as His forthcoming bride. The Millennium Church will be a Maiden Church that will be self-humbling, submit to The Holy Spirit, and come out from among the world and be separate! We must remain unspotted from the world as James instructs us to do! The maiden/ servant-hood mentality says, "What can I do to serve you today, Master?" (Leadership Bible, NIV).

That is The Millennium Maiden Church! Prepare thyself. Yield yourself as Mary did. Adorn thyself as Esther. Keep the anointing shining brightly as did the five Wise Virgins, and The Millennium Church will be the honored guest at the wedding celebration. This Millennium Maiden Church will have an ear for music – when the trumpet of the Lord shall sound there will be a distinction in that sound and she will rise to be with the Lord. She will have an ear to hear what the Spirit has to say to the church and proclaim it from the housetops. Let us prepare ourselves as The Millennium Church for the Marriage Supper of the Lamb!

Rev. Mrs. Kathy Sandlin

The Wedding Song

An Anthem for a Kings Wedding

This composition is part of the pageantry and pomp of a royal wedding. No one knows for whom it was written, yet it parallels to the Song of Solomon. Psalm 45 ultimately looks beyond earthly matrimony to the future heavenly wedding of the King of Kings, the Lord Jesus, and His bride the church. (Word in Life Study Bible – New King James Version)

For the choir director: A psalm of the descendants of Korah, to be sung to the tune "Lilies."

A love song. My heart overflows with a beautiful thought! I will recite a lovely poem to the king, for my tongue is like the pen of a skillful poet. You are the most handsome of all. Gracious words stream from your lips. God himself has blessed you forever. Put on your sword, O mighty warrior! You are so glorious, so majestic! In your majesty, ride out to victory, defending truth, humility, and justice. Go forth to perform awe-inspiring deeds! Your arrows are sharp, piercing your enemies' hearts. The nations fall before you, lying down beneath your feet. Your throne, O God, endures forever and ever. Your royal power is expressed in justice. You love what is right and hate what is wrong. Therefore God, your God, has anointed you, pouring out the oil of joy on you more than on anyone else. Your robes are perfumed with myrrh, aloes, and cassia. In palaces decorated with ivory, you are entertained by the music of harps. King's daughters are among your concubines. At your right side stands the queen, wearing jewelry of finest gold from Ophir! Listen to me, O royal daughter; take to heart what I say. Forget your people and your homeland far away. For your royal husband delights in your beauty; honor him, for he is your lord. The princes of Tyre will shower you with gifts. People of great wealth will entreat your favor. The bride, a princess, waits within her chamber, dressed in a gown woven with gold. In her beautiful robes, she is led to the king, accompanied by her bridesmaids. What a joyful, enthusiastic procession as they enter the king's palace! Your sons will become kings like their father. You will make them rulers over many lands. I will bring honor to your name in every generation. Therefore, the nations will praise you forever and ever. (Psalm 45, NIV)

REFERENCES

Word in Life Study Bible – New King James Version by Nelson Publishers

The Leadership Bible – New International Version by Zondervan Publishing House

Spirit Filled Life Bible – New King James Version by Nelson Publishers

Complete Jewish Bible – An English Version of the Old and New Testament by Jewish New Testament Publications Incorporated

Hebrew/Greek Key Study Bible – New American Standard by A M G Publishers

For more information on other resources from
Prophetess Kathy Sandlin

International Cathedral of Prayer
Post Office Box 938
Greer, South Carolina 29652

E Mail: icopprayercenter@aol.com